Rick.

POC

PRAGUE

Rick Steves & Honza Vihan with Gene Openshaw

Contents

Introduction

Few cities can match Prague's over-the-top romance, evocative Old World charm...and tourist crowds. Residents call their town "Praha" (PRAH-hah). It's big, with about 1.3 million people. But during a quick visit, you'll focus on its relatively compact old center.

Prague is equal parts historic and fun. As the only major Central European capital to escape the large-scale bombing of the last century's wars, it's one of Europe's best-preserved cities. It's a city of willowy Art Nouveau facades, Mozart concerts, and some of the best beer in Europe. Wind through walkable neighborhoods, cross the famous statue-lined Charles Bridge, and hike up to the world's biggest castle for sweeping views of the city's spires and domes. You'll see rich remnants of the city's strong Jewish heritage and stark reminders of the communist era. And you'll meet today's vibrant mix of locals and expats. Prague itself seems a work of art.

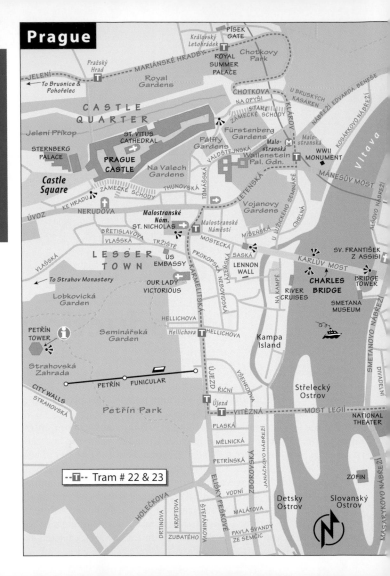

Prague

Tram # 22 & 23

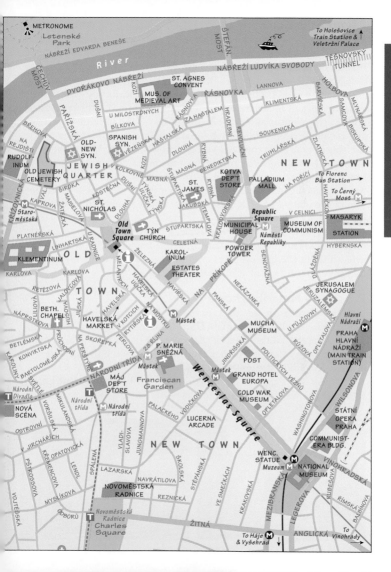

About This Book

Rick Steves Pocket Prague is a personal tour guide...in your pocket. The core of the book is five self-guided walks and tours that zero in on Prague's greatest sights and experiences.

My Old Town & Charles Bridge Walk introduces you to the city and its main sights. The Jewish Quarter Tour leads you through the synagogues and museums of Europe's best-preserved former Jewish ghetto. The Wenceslas Square Walk shows off the glitzier New Town and recalls Prague's tumultuous years under communist rule and its exciting liberation in the 1989 Velvet Revolution. The Mucha Museum Tour showcases works by the greatest modern Czech artist, Alphonse Mucha, who harnessed the slinky energy of an emerging style called Art Nouveau. And the Prague Castle Tour focuses on the most important of the many sights in this historic complex, including the towering St. Vitus Cathedral.

The rest of this book is a traveler's tool kit, with my best advice on how to save money, plan your time, use public transportation, and avoid lines at the busiest sights. You'll also get recommendations on hotels, restaurants, and activities.

Prague by Neighborhood

The Vltava River divides the city in two. East of the river are the Old Town and New Town, the main train station, and most of my recommended hotels. To the west of the river is Prague Castle and, below that, the sleepy Lesser Town. Connecting the two halves are several bridges, including the landmark Charles Bridge.

Think of Prague as a collection of neighborhoods. Until about 1800, Prague was four distinct towns with four distinct personalities.

Prague is a city of quaint neighborhoods.

The Old Town Square is the historic center.

Prague Neighborhoods

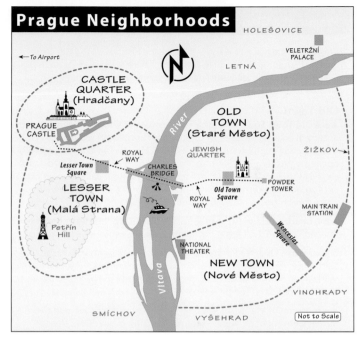

Old Town (Staré Město): Nestled in the bend of the river, this is the historic core, where most tourists spend their time. It's pedestrian-friendly, with small winding streets, old buildings, shops, and beer halls and cafés. In the center sits the charming Old Town Square. Slicing east-west through the Old Town is the main pedestrian axis, along Celetná and Karlova streets.

Jewish Quarter (Josefov): Within the Old Town, this area by the river contains a high concentration of sights from Prague's deep Jewish heritage, as well as the city's glitziest shopping area.

New Town (Nové Město): Stretching south from the Old Town is the long, broad expanse of Wenceslas Square, marking the center of the New Town. As the name implies, it's the neighborhood for modern buildings, fancy department stores, and a few communist-era sights.

Castle Quarter (Hradčany): High atop a hill on the west side of

Prague at a Glance

Prague is a fine place to wander around and just take in the fun atmosphere. Plan some worthwhile activities: Take a self-guided tram tour (page 120), hire a local guide (page 132), enjoy a concert (page 139), or go for a scenic paddle on the river (page 120).

Old Town

▲▲▲**Old Town Square** Magical main square of Old World Prague, with dozens of colorful facades, dramatic Jan Hus Memorial, looming Týn Church, and fanciful Astronomical Clock. **Hours:** Týn Church generally open to sightseers Tue-Sat 10:00-13:00 & 15:00-17:00, Sun 10:30-12:00, closed Mon; Astronomical Clock strikes on the hour daily 9:00-23:00, until 20:00 in winter; clock tower open Tue-Sun 9:00-21:00, Mon from 11:00, shorter hours Jan-March. See page 13.

▲▲▲**Charles Bridge** Atmospheric, statue-lined bridge that connects the Old Town to the Lesser Town and Prague Castle. See page 36.

▲▲▲**Jewish Quarter** Finest collection of Jewish sights in Europe, featuring various synagogues and an evocative cemetery. **Hours:** Most sights open Sun-Fri 9:00-18:00, Nov-March until 16:30, closed Sat and on Jewish holidays. See page 39.

▲▲**Museum of Medieval Art** Best Gothic art in the country, at the former Convent of St. Agnes. **Hours:** Tue-Sun 10:00-18:00, closed Mon. See page 113.

▲**Havelská Market** Colorful open-air market that sells crafts and produce. **Hours:** Daily 9:00-18:00. See page 111.

▲**Klementinum** National Library's lavish Baroque Hall and Observatory Tower (with views); visit by tour only. **Hours:** Tours daily every half-hour 10:00-17:30, shorter hours off-season. See page 111.

New Town

▲▲▲**Wenceslas Square** Lively boulevard at the heart of modern Prague. See page 59.

▲▲**Municipal House** Pure Art Nouveau architecture, including Prague's largest concert hall and several eateries. **Hours:** Daily 10:00-18:00, but most of the interior is viewable by tour only. See page 118.

▲**Cold War Museum** Re-creation of a nuclear-fallout shelter, in the basement of a hotel. **Hours:** English tours daily at 11:00, 13:00, 14:30, and 16:00. See page 116.

▲**Mucha Museum** Easy-to-appreciate collection of Art Nouveau works by Czech artist Alphonse Mucha. **Hours:** Daily 10:00-18:00. See page 73.

▲**Museum of Communism** The rise and fall of the regime, from start to Velvet finish. **Hours:** Daily 9:00-20:00. See page 117.

▲**National Memorial to the Heroes of the Heydrich Terror** Tribute to members of the resistance, who assassinated a notorious Nazi architect of the Holocaust. **Hours:** Tue-Sun 9:00-17:00, closed Mon. See page 122.

Lesser Town
▲**Petřín Hill** Lesser Town hill with public art, a funicular, and a replica of the Eiffel Tower. **Hours:** Funicular—daily 8:00-22:00; tower—daily 9:00-21:00, shorter hours off-season. See page 125.

Castle Quarter
▲▲▲**St. Vitus Cathedral** The Czech Republic's most important church, featuring a climbable tower and a striking stained-glass window by Art Nouveau artist Alphonse Mucha. **Hours:** Daily 9:00-17:00, Nov-March until 16:00, closed Sunday mornings for Mass. See page 126.

▲▲**Prague Castle** Traditional seat of Czech rulers, with St. Vitus Cathedral, Old Royal Palace, Basilica of St. George, shop-lined Golden Lane, and lots of crowds. **Hours:** Castle sights—daily 9:00-17:00, Nov-March until 16:00; castle grounds—daily 6:00-22:00. See page 83.

▲▲**Lobkowicz Palace** Delightful private art collection of a Czech noble family. **Hours:** Daily 10:00-18:00. See page 127.

▲**Strahov Monastery and Library** Baroque center of learning, with ornate reading rooms and old-fashioned science exhibits. **Hours:** Daily 9:00-12:00 & 13:00-17:00. See page 127.

▲**Loreta Church** Beautiful Baroque church, a pilgrim magnet for centuries, containing what some believe to be part of Mary's house from Nazareth. **Hours:** Daily 9:00-17:00, Nov-March 9:30-16:00. See page 129.

the river stands the massive complex of Prague Castle, marked by the spires of St. Vitus Cathedral. The surrounding area is noble and leafy, with grand buildings, little commerce, and few pubs.

Lesser Town (Malá Strana): Nestled at the foot of Castle Hill is this pleasant former town of fine palaces and gardens (and a few minor sights).

Outside the Center: A short ride away on public transit, you'll find Vyšehrad park, a good place to escape tourist crowds. Or take a day to explore some of the interesting sights that lie beyond the city's boundaries.

Planning Your Time

The following day plans give an idea of how much an organized, motivated, and caffeinated person can see. Prague deserves at least two full sightseeing days, and you might want to consider other side trips.

Day 1: Take my Old Town Walk to get oriented to the city's core. Have lunch in the Old Town or Lesser Town. Explore the Lesser Town. In midafternoon, follow my Jewish Quarter Tour. In the evening (tonight or other nights), consider a beer hall, live music, Black Light Theater, or a Metro ride to Vyšehrad park for a crowd-free stroll.

Day 2: In the morning, follow my Prague Castle Tour (see that chapter for strategies on avoiding lines and crowds). Have lunch near the castle or in the Lesser Town, then take the Metro to the Muzeum stop (at the National Museum) and do my Wenceslas Square Walk (and pop in to the Cold War Museum). Tour the Mucha Museum.

Day 3: Choose from any number of museums (see the Sights chapter for ideas), such as the Museum of Medieval Art, the Heydrich Terror memorial, or the Museum of Communism, or ascend the Old Town Hall tower for views.

With More Time: Consider a day trip to Kutná Hora, Terezín, or Karlštejn Castle (see page 130).

When to Go

The tourist season runs roughly from Easter through October, peaking in May, June, and September. July and August have the warmest weather and more daylight hours. Prague never really quiets down; winter travelers find the concert season in full swing and somewhat fewer crowds.

Rick's Free Audio Tours and Video Clips

Rick Steves Audio Europe, a free app, makes it easy to download my audio tours and listen to them offline as you travel. For this book (look for the ∩), free audio tours cover my Prague City Walk. The app also offers my public radio show interviews with travel experts from around the globe. Scan the QR code on the inside front cover to find it in your app store, or visit RickSteves.com/AudioEurope.

Rick Steves Classroom Europe, a powerful tool for teachers, is also useful for travelers. This video library contains about 600 short clips excerpted from my public television series. Enjoy these videos as you sort through options for your trip and to better understand what you'll see in Europe. Check it out at Classroom.RickSteves.com.

Before You Go

You'll have a smoother trip if you tackle a few things ahead of time. For more details on these topics, see the Practicalities chapter and RickSteves.com, which has helpful travel-tip articles and videos.

Make sure your travel documents are valid. If your passport is due to expire within six months of your ticketed date of return, you need to renew it. Allow 12 weeks or more to renew or get a passport. Be aware of any entry requirements; you may need to register with the European Travel Information and Authorization System (ETIAS) before you travel (quick and easy process; check https://travel-europe.europa.eu/etias_en). Get passport and country-specific travel info at Travel.State.gov.

Arrange your transportation. Book your international flights. Figure out your transportation options. If traveling beyond Prague, research train reservations, rail passes, and car rentals.

Book rooms well in advance, especially if your trip falls during peak season or any major holidays or festivals.

Reserve ahead for key sights. Several castles (Konopiště and Karlštejn) require you to reserve a day or so ahead for a spot on a guided tour to visit all or part of the interior; request an English tour.

Consider travel insurance. Compare the cost of insurance to the cost of your potential loss. Understand what protections your credit card might offer and whether your existing insurance (health, homeowners, or renters) covers you and your possessions overseas.

Manage your money. "Tap-to-pay" or "contactless" cards are widely accepted and simple to use. You may need your card's PIN for some purchases—request it if you don't have one. Alert your bank that you'll be using your cards in Europe. You don't need to bring Czech crowns; you can withdraw them from ATMs in Europe.

Use your smartphone smartly. Sign up for an international service plan to reduce your costs, or rely on Wi-Fi in Europe instead. Download any apps you'll want on the road, such as maps, translators, and Rick Steves Audio Europe (see sidebar).

Pack light. You'll walk with your luggage more than you think. I travel for weeks with a single carry-on bag and a day pack. Use the packing checklist in Practicalities as a guide.

Travel Smart

If you have a positive attitude, equip yourself with good information (this book), and expect to travel smart, you will.

Pickpockets abound in crowded places where tourists congregate. Treat commotions as smokescreens for theft. Keep your passport and backup cash and cards secure in a money belt tucked under your clothes; carry only a day's spending money and a card in your front pocket or wallet.

If you wilt easily, choose a hotel with air-conditioning, start your day early, take a midday siesta, and resume your sightseeing later.

Be sure to schedule in slack time for picnics, laundry, people-watching, leisurely dinners, shopping, and recharging your touristic batteries. Slow down and be open to unexpected experiences and the hospitality of the Czech people.

Munch on a *trdlo* in the Old Town Square, meander down twisting streets, or order a Pilsner at a local pub. As you visit places I know and love, I'm happy you'll be meeting some of my favorite Czechs.

Happy travels! *Užij si výlet!*

Old Town & Charles Bridge Walk

A boomtown since the 11th century, Prague's compact, pedestrian-friendly Old Town has long been a busy commercial quarter, filled with merchants, students, and supporters of the Church reformer Jan Hus (who wanted a Czech-style Catholicism). Today, it's Prague's tourism ground zero, jammed with tasteful landmarks and tacky amusements alike.

This walk starts in the heart of the neighborhood, the Old Town Square. From here we'll snake our way to the edge of the New Town (at Wenceslas Square), and end at the river on the atmospheric Charles Bridge. We'll see Gothic churches with Baroque interiors, Renaissance gables, Art Nouveau facades, and a curious old clock—and learn how the Czech people have courageously fought foreign oppression.

ORIENTATION

Length of This Walk: Allow three hours. It's a great overview of sights you may want to visit in depth later.

Crowd Warning: Much of this walk is packed with sightseers all day. A huge bottleneck occurs in front of the Astronomical Clock near the top of each hour.

Getting There: This walk begins right on the Old Town Square, Prague's centerpiece.

Týn Church: 40 Kč requested donation, generally open to sightseers Tue-Sat 10:00-13:00 & 15:00-17:00, Sun 10:30-12:00, closed Mon.

Old Town Hall Tower and Tour: 300 Kč for Old Town Hall and tower ascent, cheaper online; Tue-Sun 9:00-21:00, Mon from 11:00, shorter hours Jan-March; included Town Hall tours usually 4/day in English at 10:00, 12:00, 14:00, and 16:00—preregister at ticket office; www.prague.eu.

Church of St. James: Free, Tue-Sun 9:30-12:00 & 14:00-16:00, closed Mon.

Municipal House: Free to view entrance halls and public spaces; daily 10:00-18:00; tours—290 Kč, usually 3/day between 11:00-17:00.

Havelská Market: Open-air market open daily 9:00-18:00; fruit, souvenirs, puppets, and toys on weekends.

Klementinum: 300 Kč, tours depart daily every half-hour 10:00-17:30, shorter hours off-season.

Charles Bridge Tower Climb: 150 Kč, daily 9:00-21:00, April-May and Sept 10:00-19:00, Oct-March until 18:00.

Starring: Prague's showpiece main square, fine old churches, architectural landmarks, and the spunky Czech spirit.

Get a healthy snack at Havelská Market.

Enjoy the view from the Old Town Hall tower.

THE TOUR BEGINS

▶ *Plant yourself anywhere in the Old Town Square and survey the scene.*

You're standing in the center of historic Prague, a city of 1.3 million people and the capital of the Czech Republic. The vast square (worth ▲▲▲) is ringed with colorful buildings; dotted with towers, steeples, and statues; lined with cafés; and alive with people. It seems there's always something entertaining happening here.

This has been a market square since the 11th century. It became the nucleus of the Old Town (Staré Město) in the 13th century, when its Town Hall was built. In the past, it was the site of commerce, parades, demonstrations, and executions. Today, the old-time market stalls have been replaced by outdoor cafés and the tackiest breed of souvenir stands. But you're surrounded by plenty of history.

▶ *Begin with the square's centerpieces, the...*

❶ Jan Hus and Virgin Mary Monuments

The first monument, the **Jan Hus Memorial,** was erected in 1915 and is an enduring icon of the long struggle for (Czech) freedom. In the center, Jan Hus—the reformer who became the symbol of Czech nationalism—stands tall amid the rising flames. Hus, born in 1369, was a priest who challenged both the Church's and the secular rulers' claim to dominion. His defiant stance—depicted so powerfully in this monument—galvanized the Czech people, who rallied to fight not just for their religious beliefs but for independence from any man-made (rather than natural, or God-given) controls.

But Hus was centuries ahead of his time. He was arrested,

The Old Town Square still feels old.

Jan Hus, symbol of Czech nationalism

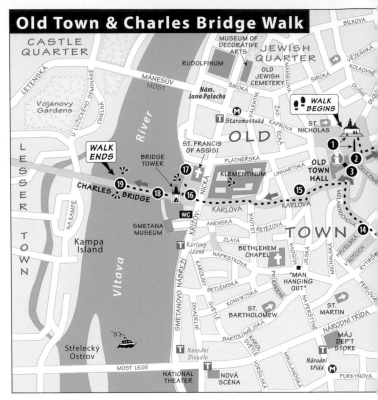

Old Town & Charles Bridge Walk

charged with heresy, excommunicated, and, in 1415, burned at the stake. His followers, called Hussites, picked up the torch and fought on for two decades in the Hussite Wars, which killed tens of thousands and left Bohemia a virtual wasteland.

Surrounding Hus' statue are the Hussites who battled the entrenched powers of their time. One patriot holds a cup, or chalice. This symbolizes one of the changes the Hussites were fighting for: the right of everyone (not just priests) to drink the wine at Communion. Two hundred years later, in 1620, a disorganized Czech rebellion was crushed by the united Habsburgs at White Mountain just outside

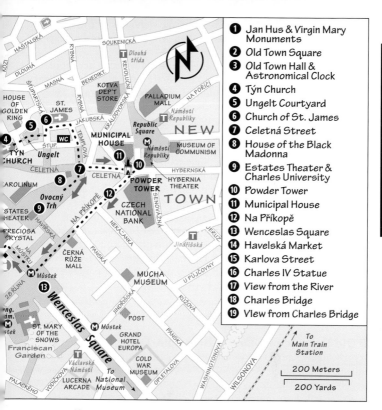

1. Jan Hus & Virgin Mary Monuments
2. Old Town Square
3. Old Town Hall & Astronomical Clock
4. Týn Church
5. Ungelt Courtyard
6. Church of St. James
7. Celetná Street
8. House of the Black Madonna
9. Estates Theater & Charles University
10. Powder Tower
11. Municipal House
12. Na Příkopě
13. Wenceslas Square
14. Havelská Market
15. Karlova Street
16. Charles IV Statue
17. View from the River
18. Charles Bridge
19. View from Charles Bridge

Prague—effectively ending Czech independence and freedom of worship for three centuries.

But the story ends well. Huddled just behind Jan Hus are a mother and her children—prophesizing the ultimate rebirth of the Czech nation. And indeed, three years after the statue was unveiled, the Czechs regained their political independence.

Each subsequent age has interpreted Hus to its liking: For Protestants, Hus was the founder of the first Protestant church (though he was actually an ardent Catholic); for revolutionaries, this critic of the temporal powers was a proponent of social equality; for nationalists, this Czech preacher was the defender of the language; and for communists, this ideologue was first to preach the gospel of communal ownership.

Now turn your attention to the **Virgin Mary** atop her sandstone column. Originally erected in 1652, shortly after the Thirty Years' War, the first genuinely Baroque statue in Prague honored Mary as the city's protector. Mary was intended to rally Catholics and non-Catholics alike. But by the late 19th century, ardent nationalists had come to perceive this delicate, Bernini-inspired Mary as a symbol of the militantly Catholic Habsburgs. A few days after the declaration of independence in 1918, a rebellious mob turned on the "Habsburg" Virgin, tearing down the column and breaking the statue. But pious Catholics felt a sense of injustice: Isn't Mary a symbol of unity and peace?

Under communism there was little chance to restore the monument, but the debate resurfaced after 1989. For 23 years Czech sculptor Petr Váňa worked on a faithful replica. Finally, in 2020, Prague's city council allowed the Virgin to return to her original spot, reigniting the century-old controversy. It will take time for Prague's citizens to get used to having two monuments in the square.

▶ *Stepping away from the monuments, stand in the center of the Old Town Square, and take a 360-degree...*

❷ Old Town Square Orientation Spin-Tour

Whirl clockwise to get a look at Prague's diverse architectural styles: Gothic, Renaissance, Baroque, Rococo, and Art Nouveau. Prague was largely spared the devastating aerial bombardments of World War II that leveled so many European cities (like Berlin, Warsaw, and Budapest). Few places can match the Old Town Square for Old World charm.

Start with the green domes of the Baroque **Church of St. Nicholas.** Originally Catholic, now Hussite, this church is a popular concert venue. The Jewish Quarter is a few blocks behind the church, down the uniquely tree-lined "Paris Street" (Pařížská)—which also has the best lineup of Art Nouveau houses in Prague.

Spin to the right. Behind the Hus Memorial is a fine yellow building that introduces us to Prague's wonderful world of Art Nouveau: pastel colors, fanciful stonework, wrought-iron balconies, colorful murals—and what are those firemen statues on top doing? Prague's architecture is a wonderland of ornamental details.

Continue spinning a few doors to the right to the large, red-and-tan Rococo **Kinský Palace,** which displays the National Gallery's top-notch temporary exhibits.

Immediately to the right of the Rococo palace stands the tower-like **House by the Bell,** one of the finest examples of a 13th-century Gothic patrician house anywhere in Europe (also the oldest building on the square).

Farther to the right is the towering, Gothic **Týn Church** (pron. "teen"), with its fanciful twin spires. It's been the Old Town's leading church in every era. In medieval times, it was Catholic. When the Hussites came to dominate the city (c. 1420s), they made it the headquarters of their faith. After the Habsburg victory in 1620, it reverted to Catholicism. The symbolism tells the story: Between the church's two towers, find a golden medallion of the Virgin Mary. Beneath that is a niche with a golden chalice. In Hussite times, the chalice symbolized their cause—that all should be able to take Communion. When the Catholics triumphed, they melted down the original chalice and made it into the golden image of Mary. In 2016, the chalice—with the Communion wafer added to dispel any Hussite symbolism—was returned to the niche.

The row of pastel houses in front of Týn Church has a mixture of Gothic, Renaissance, and Baroque facades and gables. If you like live music, the convenient **Via Musica box office** near the church's front door has all the concert options; we'll pass it later on this walk.

Spinning right, to the south side of the square, take in more **glorious facades,** each a different color with a different gable on top—step gables, triangular, bell-shaped. The tan 19th-century Neo-Gothic house at #16 has a steepled bay window and a mural of St. Wenceslas on horseback.

Finally, you reach the pointed 250-foot-tall spire marking the 14th-century **Old Town Hall.**

Approach the Old Town Hall and notice at the base of the tower, near the corner of the tree-filled park, the **27 white crosses** inlaid in the pavement. These mark the spot where 27 nobles, merchants, and intellectuals—Protestants *and* Catholics—were beheaded in 1621 after

Týn Church's towers are a symbol of the city.

the White Mountain defeat. This is still considered one of the grimmest chapters in the country's history.

▶ *Around the left side of the tower are two big, fancy, old clock faces, being admired by many, many tourists.*

❸ Old Town Hall and Astronomical Clock

The Old Town Hall, with its distinctive trapezoidal tower, was built in the 1350s, during Prague's golden age. The ornately carved Gothic entrance door to the left of the clock leads to the TI, a pay WC, and the ticket desk for the clock tower elevator and Old Town Hall tours (described on page 110). First, turn your attention to the famous **Astronomical Clock.** See if you can figure out how it works. Of the two giant dials on the tower, the top one tells the time. It has a complex series of revolving wheels within wheels, but the basics are simple.

The two big, outer dials tell the time in a 24-hour circle. Of these, the inner dial is stationary and is marked with the Roman numerals I-XII twice, starting at the top and bottom of the dial—noon and midnight. The colorful background of this dial indicates the amount of daylight at different times of day: The black circle surrounded by orange at the bottom half (from XII "p.m." to IV "a.m.") is nighttime, while the blue top half is daytime, and the shades of gray and orange between them represent dawn and dusk.

Meanwhile, the outer dial (with the golden numbers on a black band) lists the numbers 1 through 24, in a strange but readable Bohemian script. But because this uses the medieval Italian method of telling time—where the day resets at sunset—the 1 is not at the top, but somewhere in the lower-right quadrant of the Roman dial. The Roman numeral that the Bohemian 1 lines up with tells you the time of last night's sunset (typically between IV and VIII "p.m.").

The "big hand" (with the golden sun on it) does one slow sweep each 24-hour period, marking the time on both dials.

Now pay attention to the offset inner ring, marked with the zodiac signs. This ring both rotates on its own and moves around the outer dial, so the sunny "big hand" also lands on today's zodiac sign. And the "little hand" (with a blue moon) appears in this month's zodiac.

The second dial, below the clock, was added in the 19th century. It shows the signs of the zodiac, scenes from the seasons of a rural peasant's life, and a ring of saints' names. There's one for each day of the year, and a marker on top indicates today's special saint. In the center is a castle, symbolizing Prague.

Four statues flank the upper clock. These politically incorrect symbols evoke a 15th-century outlook: The figure staring into a mirror stands for vanity, a Jewish moneylender holding a bag of coins is greed, and (on the right side) a Turk with a mandolin symbolizes hedonism. All these worldly goals are vain in the face of Death, whose hourglass reminds us that our time is unavoidably running out.

The clock strikes the top of the hour and puts on a little **glockenspiel show** daily from 9:00 to 23:00 (until 20:00 in winter). As the hour approaches, keep your eye on Death. First, Death tips his hourglass and pulls the cord, ringing the bell, while the moneylender jingles his purse. Then the windows open and the 12 apostles shuffle past, acknowledging the gang of onlookers. Finally, the rooster at the very top crows and the hour is rung. The hour is often wrong because of Daylight Saving Time (completely senseless to 15th-century clockmakers). I find an alternative view just as interesting: As the cock crows, face the crowd and snap a photo of the mass of gaping tourists.

▸ *Now head back across the square to tour the pointy Týn Church. Enter by making your way through the cluster of buildings in front of it. (If*

Ponder the wheels-within-wheels and intriguing artwork of the fascinating Astronomical Clock.

A Little Walking History

As you're walking through living Czech history, you'll note a theme that runs throughout: The tiny Czech nation has had to constantly fight to survive amid more powerful neighbors.

The nation was born under the duke Wenceslas, who unified the Czech people 1,100 years ago. Prague's medieval golden age peaked under Charles IV (c. 1350), who built many of the city's best-known monuments.

Over the next centuries, the Czechs were forever struggling to maintain their proud heritage. First, they defied the pope, led by religious reformer Jan Hus. Then they chafed under the yoke of the Austrian Habsburgs. Finally, in the historic year 1918, the modern nation of Czechoslovakia was created. Unfortunately, that nation was trampled yet again—first by Nazis, then by the communist Soviet Union. In 1989, huge protests peacefully tossed out the communists in the Velvet Revolution.

Rising nationalist feelings in Slovakia in the early 1990s helped lead to the peaceful dissolution of Czechoslovakia into the Czech Republic and Slovakia on January 1, 1993. In 1999, both countries joined NATO, followed in 2004 by the EU.

the church is closed, try peeking in from the locked gate just inside the door.)

❹ Týn Church

This is the Old Town's main church (worth ▲). While it has roots dating back to the 1100s, this structure dates from Prague's golden age. It was built around 1360 as the university church by the same architect who designed St. Vitus Cathedral at Prague Castle.

The interior is full of light, with soaring Gothic arches. The ornamentation reflects the church's troubled history. Originally Catholic, it was taken over by the Hussites, who whitewashed it and stripped it of Catholic icons. When the Catholic Habsburgs retook the church, they redecorated with a vengeance—encrusting its once elegant and pure Gothic columns with ornate Baroque altars and statues of Mary and the saints.

Now do a slow, counterclockwise tour around the church, heading up the right aisle.

At the front-right corner of the church (to the right of the pulpit), on the pillar, is a brown stone slab showing an armored man with a beard and ruff collar, his hand resting on a globe. This is the first modern astronomer, **Tycho Brahe** (1546-1601). Buried here, he was brought to Prague by the Habsburgs.

Now circle around to face the stunning **main altar,** topped with a statue of the archangel Michael with a flaming sword. A painting (on the lower level) shows Mary ascending to heaven where (in the next painting up) she's to be crowned.

To the right of the altar is a statue of one of Prague's patron saints, **John of Nepomuk**—always easy to identify thanks to his halo of stars (we'll learn more about him later in the walk).

You're surrounded by the **double-eagle symbol** of the Catholic Habsburgs: on the flag borne by a knight statue on the altar, atop the organ behind you (Prague's oldest), and above you on the ceiling.

▶ *Exiting the church, walk through the **Via Musica** ticket office (on your right; a handy place to get classical music tickets). Leaving at the far end, turn right, where you'll walk by the north entrance to the Týn Church (with the most delicate pieces of Gothic stone masonry in town—all original 14th-century).*

Right behind the church, pass through an imposing gate into the courtyard called the Ungelt, what was once the commercial nucleus of medieval Prague.

❺ Ungelt Courtyard

This quiet, pleasant, cobbled courtyard of upscale restaurants and shops is one of the Old Town's oldest places. During the Bohemian golden age (c. 1200-1400), the Ungelt was a multicultural hub of international trade. Prague—located at the geographical center of Europe—attracted Germans selling furs, Italians selling fine art, Frenchmen selling cloth, and Arabs selling spices. They converged on this

Ungelt courtyard, for medieval merchants

St. James, the Old Town's best interior

courtyard, where they could store their goods and pay their customs (which is what *Ungelt* means, in German). In return, the king granted them protection, housing, and a stable for their horses. By day, they'd sell their wares on the Old Town Square. At night, they'd return here to drink and exchange news from their native lands. Notice that, to protect the goods, there are only two entrances to the complex. After centuries of disuse, the Ungelt has been marvelously restored—a great place for dinner, and a reminder that Prague has been a cosmopolitan center for most of its history.

▸ *Exit the Ungelt at the far end. Just to your left, across the street, is the...*

❻ Church of St. James (Kostel Sv. Jakuba)

Perhaps the most beautiful church interior in the Old Town, the Church of St. James (worth ▲) has been the home of the Minorite Order almost as long as merchants have occupied the Ungelt. A medieval city was a complex phenomenon: Commerce and a life of contemplation existed side by side.

Artistically, St. James is a stunning example of how simple medieval spaces could be rebuilt into sumptuous feasts of Baroque decoration. The original interior was destroyed by fire in 1689; what's here now is an early 18th-century remodel. The blue light in the altar highlights one of Prague's most venerated treasures—the bejeweled Madonna Pietatis. Above the pietà, as if held aloft by hummingbird-like angels, is a painting of the martyrdom of St. James.

Proceed grandly up the central aisle, enjoying a parade of gilded statues and paintings under a colorfully frescoed ceiling telling stories of the Virgin Mary's life. When you reach the altar at the front, turn around and notice how the church suddenly becomes simpler without all that ornamentation. Prague's grandest pipe organ fills the back wall.

As you leave, look for the black, shriveled-up arm with clenched fingers (hanging by a chain from a metal post 15 feet above and to the left of the door). According to legend, a thief attempted to rob the Madonna Pietatis from the altar, but his hand was frozen the moment he touched the statue. The monks had to cut off his arm to get the hand to let go. The desiccated arm now hangs here as a warning.

▶ *Exiting the church, do a U-turn to the left (heading up Jakubská street, along the side of the church, past some rough-looking bars). After one block, turn right on Templová street. Head two blocks down the street (passing a nice view of the Týn Church's rear end and some self-proclaimed "deluxe toilets") and go through the arcaded passageway, where you emerge onto...*

❼ Celetná Street

Since the 10th century, this street has been a corridor in the busy commercial quarter—filled with merchants and guilds. These days, it's still pretty commercial, and very touristy.

Here on Celetná street, you're surrounded by a number of buildings with striking facades. To the left is the medieval Powder Tower—we'll head there in a moment. Straight ahead of you is a Baroque balcony supported by four statues. Many facades on this street are Baroque or Neoclassical—pastel colors, with frilly or statuesque features. It's little wonder that, when filmmakers want to shoot a movie set in frilly Baroque times, they often choose Prague.

▶ *To your right is a striking, angular cinnamon-colored building called the...*

❽ House of the Black Madonna
(Dům u Černé Matky Boží)

Back around the turn of the 20th century, Prague was a center of avant-garde art. Art Nouveau blossomed here (as we'll soon see), as did Cubism. The House of the Black Madonna's Cubist exterior is a marvel of rectangular windows and cornices—stand back and see how masterfully it makes its statement while mixing with its neighbors... then get up close and study the details. The interior houses a Cubist

Celetná street has traditional shops.

Cubist-inspired House of the Black Madonna

café (the recommended Grand Café Orient, one flight up the parabolic spiral staircase)—complete with cube-shaped chairs and square rolls. The Kubista gallery in the far corner shows more examples of this unique style. This building is an example of what has long been considered the greatest virtue of Prague's architects: the ability to adapt grandiose plans to the existing cityscape.

▶ *The long, skinny square that begins just to the left of the Cubist house is the former fruit market (Ovocný Trh). For a peek at the local university and a historic theater, side-trip to the end of this square, then return to this spot.*

❾ Estates Theater and Charles University

The **Estates Theater** (Stavovské Divadlo) is the fancy green-and-white Neoclassical building at the end of the square. Built in the 1780s in a deliberately Parisian style, it was the prime opera venue in Prague at a time when an Austrian prodigy was changing the course of music. Wolfgang Amadeus Mozart premiered *Don Giovanni* in this building (with a bronze statue of Il Commendatore, a character from that opera, duly flanking the main entrance), and he directed many of his works here. Today, the theater continues to produce *The Marriage of Figaro, Don Giovanni,* and *The Magic Flute.*

The main building of Prague's **Charles University,** the Karolinum, is next door (on the right as you face the theater, tucked down a little courtyard). Imagine Prague in the late 1500s, when it was the center of the Holy Roman Empire, and one of the most enlightened places in Europe. The astronomers Tycho Brahe (who tracked the planets) and his assistant Johannes Kepler (who formulated the laws of motion) both worked here. Charles University has always been at the center of Czech political thinking and revolutions, from Jan Hus in the 15th century to the passionately patriotic Czech students who swept communists out of power in the Velvet Revolution.

The ground-floor Gothic interior of the Karolinum can be visited for free—find the modern main entrance in the little fenced-off courtyard by the lions fountain (just turn left as you walk past the guard).

▶ *Return to the House of the Black Madonna. Then turn right and head up busy Celetná street to the big, black…*

⑩ Powder Tower

The 500-year-old Powder Tower was the main gate of the old town wall. It also housed the city's gunpowder—hence the name. This is the only surviving bit of the wall that was built to defend the city in the 1400s. (Though you can go inside, it's not worth paying to tour the interior.)

The Powder Tower was the city's formal front door—the road from Vienna entered here. Picture the scene three centuries ago, when Habsburg empress Maria Theresa had finally been crowned Queen of Bohemia. As she returned home in triumph, she passed through the Powder Tower gate.

Go back 500 years and look up at the impressive Gothic-carved welcoming committee, reminding all of the hierarchy of our mortal existence: Reading from the bottom up, you'll see artisans flanking Prague's coat of arms, a pair of Czech kings with seals of alliance with neighboring regions, angels with golden wings, and saints flanking Christ in majesty. The tower is topped with one of Prague's signature styles—a trapezoidal roof.

▶ *Pass regally through the Powder Tower, leaving the Old Town. You'll*

Estates Theater—playing Mozart since the 1780s   Powder Tower—once the town's main gate

Prague: The Queen of Art Nouveau

Prague is Europe's best city for Art Nouveau, the style of art and architecture that flourished throughout Europe around 1900. It was called "nouveau"—or new—because it was associated with all things modern: technology, social progress, and enlightened thinking. Art Nouveau was

neo-nothing, but instead a fresh answer to all the revival styles of the late 19th century, and an organic response to the Eiffel Tower art of the Industrial Age.

By taking advantage of recent advances in engineering, Art Nouveau liberated the artist in each architect. Notice the curves and motifs expressing originality—every facade is unique. Artists such as Alphonse Mucha believed that the style should apply to all facets of daily life. They designed everything from buildings and furniture to typefaces and cigarette packs.

Though Art Nouveau was born in Paris, it's in Prague where you'll find some of its greatest hits: the Municipal House and nearby buildings, Grand Hotel Europa (on Wenceslas Square), the exuberant facades of the Jewish Quarter, the Jerusalem Synagogue, and—especially—the work of Mucha. You can see his stained-glass window in St. Vitus Cathedral (at Prague Castle) and his art at the excellent Mucha Museum (near Wenceslas Square).

emerge into a big, busy intersection. To your left is the Municipal House, a cream-colored building topped with a green dome. Find a spot with a good view of the facade.

⓫ Municipal House (Obecní Dům)

The Municipal House is the "pearl of Czech Art Nouveau." Art Nouveau flourished during the same period as the Eiffel Tower and Europe's great Industrial Age train stations.

The Municipal House sports Art Nouveau ironwork, murals, and statues, and has a great interior.

The same engineering prowess and technological advances that went into making those huge erector-set rigid buildings were used by artistic architects to create the opposite effect: curvy, organically flowing lines, inspired by vines and curvaceous women. Art Nouveau was a reaction to the sterility of modern-age construction. Look at the elaborate wrought-iron balcony—flanked by bronze Atlases hefting their lanterns—and the lovely stained glass (as in the entrance arcade).

Mosaics and sculptural knickknacks (see the faces above the windows) made the building's facade colorful and joyous. Study the bright mosaic above the balcony, called ***Homage to Prague.*** A symbol of the city, the goddess Praha presides over a land of peace and high culture—an image that stoked cultural pride and nationalist sentiment. On the balcony is a medallion showing the three-tower castle that is the symbol of Prague.

The Municipal House was built in the early 1900s, when Czech nationalism was at a fever pitch. Having been ruled by the Austrian Habsburgs for the previous 300 years, the Czechs were demanding independence. This building was drenched in patriotic Czech themes, and all the artists and materials used were Czech. Within a few short years, in 1918, the nation of Czechoslovakia was formed—and the independence proclamation was announced to the people right here, from the balcony of the Municipal House.

The Municipal House interior has some of Europe's finest Art Nouveau decor and is worth ▲▲. It's free to enter and wander the public areas. On a quick stop, check out the Art Nouveau café and restaurant near the entrance. (For details on visiting the Municipal House interior, see page 118.)

▶ *Now head west down Na Příkopě.*

⑫ Na Příkopě, the Old City Wall

The street called Na Příkopě was where the old city wall once stood. More specifically, the name Na Příkopě means "On the Moat," and you're walking along what was once the moat outside the wall. To your right is the Old Town; to the left, the New. Look at your city map and conceptualize medieval Prague's smart design: The city was protected on two sides by its river and on the other two sides by its walls (marked by the modern streets called Na Příkopě, Revoluční, and Národní Třída). The only river crossing back then was the fortified Charles Bridge.

Though the moat and city wall are now long gone, there's still a strong divide between the Old Town and the New Town. Na Příkopě—with its modern buildings, banks, and workaday franchise stores—is more New than Old. It's bustling and lively, without a hint of the trouble Prague endured in the mid-20th century. Many modern shopping malls hide behind protected facades along this boulevard.

Pause for a moment—immersed in all of this modern

Na Příkopě street, where the city wall stood

Wenceslas Square, hub of the New Town

commerce—and ponder the hard times under communism: Prague became a gray and bleak world of decrepit buildings. Some consumer goods were scarce—customers waited in long lines for bananas or a bottle of ersatz Coke. Statues were black with soot, and on the Charles Bridge—so busy today—there was nothing but onrushing locals and a few shady characters trying to change money. At the train station, frightened but desperate locals would meet arriving foreigners and offer to rent them a room, hoping to earn enough Western cash to buy Swiss chocolate or Levi's at one of the hard-currency stores. Life seemed hopeless. In spring 1968, the Czechs tried to rise up, enacting government reforms that came to be called "Prague Spring." But Soviet tanks rumbled into Prague and crushed the rebellion. It wasn't until a generation later, in 1989, that the sad tale finally had its happy ending...and it happened just steps away from here, at our next stop.

▶ *Continue up Na Příkopě to an intersection (and nearby Metro stop) called Můstek. To your left stretches the vast expanse of the wide boulevard called...*

⑬ Wenceslas Square

Wenceslas Square—with the National Museum and landmark statue of St. Wenceslas at the very top—is the centerpiece of Prague's New Town (rated ▲▲▲). This square was originally founded as a thriving horse market. Today it's a modern world of high-fashion stores, glitzy shopping malls, fine old facades (and some jarringly modern ones), fast-food restaurants, and sausage stands.

Picture the scene on this square on a cold November night in 1989: The Berlin Wall had fallen, and a student protest in Prague had been put down violently—the last straw for a city that was fed up with the oppressive communist system. Each night for two weeks, hundreds of thousands of freedom-loving Czechs filled Wenceslas Square, jingling their key chains as a sign that it was time for their overlords to pack up and go home. Finally, the formerly jailed playwright Václav Havel appeared on a balcony to announce the end of communism. The crowd celebrated wildly, having overthrown the rule of an "Evil Empire" without firing a shot...a feat that has come to be known as the Velvet Revolution. (📖 For more on the Velvet Revolution, landmarks of Wenceslas Square, and the New Town, see the Wenceslas Square Walk chapter.)

▶ *Let's plunge back into the Old Town and return to the Old Town Square. Turn around, and with your back to Wenceslas Square, head downhill on the street called Na Můstku—"along the bridge"—that crossed the moat (příkopě) we've been following until now. After one touristy block, Na Můstku jogs slightly to the left and becomes Melantrichova.*

Ahead, on the next corner, is **Preciosa House of Czech Crystal,** *established in Bohemia in 1724. The shop's awe-inspiring chandeliers invite you to step in and browse, and its staff is evangelical about showing visitors around. A block farther along, on the left, is the thriving...*

⓮ Havelská Market

This open-air market, offering crafts and produce, was first set up in the 13th century for the German trading community. Though heavy on souvenirs these days, the market (worth ▲) still feeds hungry locals and vagabonds. Lined with inviting benches, it's an ideal place to enjoy a healthy snack—and merchants are happy to sell a single vegetable or piece of fruit. The market is also a fun place to browse for crafts. It's a homegrown, homemade kind of place; you may be dealing with the actual artist or farmer. The cafés in the old arcades offer a relaxing vantage point from which to view the action.

▶ *Continue along Melantrichova street. At the Astronomical Clock, turn left down Karlova street. The rest of our walk follows Karlova to the Charles Bridge. Begin by heading along the top of the Small Market Square (Malé Náměstí, with lots of outdoor tables), then follow Karlova's twisting course—Karlova street signs keep you on track, and Karlův Most signs point to the bridge. Or just go generally downhill and follow the crowds.*

Havelská Market—produce, gifts, people

Karlova street, the (crowded) main drag

⓯ Karlova Street

Although traffic-free, Karlova street is utterly jammed with tourists as it winds toward the Charles Bridge. But the route has plenty of historic charm if you're able to ignore the contemporary tourism. As you walk, look up. Notice historic symbols and signs of shops, which advertised who lived there or what they sold. Cornerstones, designed to protect buildings from careening carriages, also date from centuries past.

The touristy feeding-frenzy of today's Prague is at its ugliest along this commercial gauntlet. Obviously, you'll find few good values on this drag. The many charming stalls selling *trdlo* (chimney cakes) imply that they are a Czech tradition. But they're just another gimmick, imported from Hungary in the last few years, to snare a little of that tourist money.

The **Klementinum** (which once housed Charles University's library) is the large building that borders Karlova street on the right. Just past the intersection with Liliová, where the street opens into a little square, turn right through the archway (at #1) and into a tranquil courtyard that feels an eternity away from the touristy hubbub of Karlova. You can also visit the Klementinum's impressive ▲ Baroque interior on a guided tour (see page 111).

▶ *Karlova street leads directly to a tall medieval tower that marks the start of Charles Bridge. But before entering the bridge, stop on this side of the river. To the right of the tower is a little park with a great view of both the bridge and the rest of Prague across the river.*

⓰ Charles IV Statue: The Bohemian Golden Age

Start with the statue of the bridge's namesake, Charles IV (1316-1378). Look familiar? He's the guy on the 100-koruna bill. Charles was the Holy Roman Emperor who ruled his vast empire from Prague in the 14th century—a high-water mark in the city's history. The statue shows one of Charles' many accomplishments: He holds a contract establishing Charles University, the first in Central Europe. The women around the pedestal symbolize the school's four traditional subjects: theology, the arts, law, and medicine.

Charles was the preeminent figure in Europe in the late Middle Ages, and the father of the Prague we enjoy today. His domain encompassed the modern Czech Republic, and parts of Germany, Austria, Italy, and the Low Countries.

Charles was cosmopolitan. Born in Prague, raised in Paris, crowned in Rome, and inspired by the luxury-loving pope in Avignon, Charles returned home bringing Europe's culture with him. Besides founding Charles University, he built Charles Bridge, much of Prague Castle and St. Vitus Cathedral, and the New Town (modeled on Paris). His Golden Bull of 1356 served as Europe's constitution for centuries (and gave anti-Semite Charles first right to the Jews' property). Power-hungry, he expanded his empire through networking and shrewd marriages, not war. Charles traded ideas with the Italian poet Petrarch and imported artists from France, Italy, and Flanders (inspiring the art of the Museum of Medieval Art—described in the Sights chapter). Under Charles, Prague became the most cultured city in Europe.

Now look up at the **bridge tower** (climb it for wonderful views—see page 112). Built by Charles, it's one of the finest Gothic gates anywhere. The statuary shows the 14th-century hierarchy of society: people at street level, above them kings, and bishops above the kings.

▶ *Stroll to the riverside, belly up to the banister, and take in the...*

⓱ View from the River

Before you are the Vltava River and Charles Bridge. Across the river, atop the hill, is Prague Castle topped by the prickly spires of St. Vitus Cathedral. **Prague Castle** has been the seat of power in this region for over a thousand years, since the time of Wenceslas. By some measures, it's the biggest castle on earth. Given the castle's long history, it's no wonder that, when the nation of Czechoslovakia was formed in 1918, Prague Castle served as the "White House" of its new president. If you tour the castle, you also get access to historic St. Vitus Cathedral,

Charles IV made Prague a world capital.

View of the hill-topping castle complex

which was begun by Charles IV. The cathedral has the tomb of Wenceslas as well as a stunning Art Nouveau stained-glass window by Alphonse Mucha. (📖 For details, see the Prague Castle Tour chapter.)

The **Vltava River** (from Old German "wild waters") is better known by the modern German mutation of the same name, Moldau. It bubbles up from the Šumava Hills in southern Bohemia and runs 270 miles through a diverse landscape, like a thread connecting the Czech people. As we've learned, the Czechs have struggled heroically to carve out their identity while surrounded by mightier neighbors—Austrians, Germans, and Russians. The Vltava is their shared artery.

The **view of Charles Bridge** from here is supremely photogenic. The historic stone bridge, commissioned in 1342, connects the Old Town with the district called the Lesser Town at the base of the castle across the river. The bridge is almost seven football fields long, lined with lanterns and 30 statues, and bookmarked at each end with medieval towers (both climbable).

▶ *Now wander onto the bridge. Make your way slowly across the bridge, checking out several of the statues, all on the right-hand side.*

⓲ Charles Bridge (Karlův Most)

Among Prague's defining landmarks, this much-loved ▲▲▲ bridge offers one of the most pleasant and entertaining strolls in Europe. Musicians, artisans, and a constant parade of people make it a festival every day. You can return to this bridge throughout the day to enjoy its various charms. Early and late, it can be enchantingly lonely. It's a photographer's delight during that "magic hour," when the sun is low in the sky.

The impressively expressive statues on either side of the bridge depict saints. Today, most of these statues are replicas—the originals are in city museums, safe from the polluted air.

Pause at the **third statue** on the right. Originally, there were no statues on the bridge, only a cross. You can still see that cross incorporated into this crucifixion scene. The rest of the bridge's statues were added when the Habsburg Catholics ruled in the 17th and 18th centuries. After the Hussite years, the Habsburgs wanted to make sure the saints overlooked and inspired the townsfolk each day as they crossed what was still the only bridge in town.

Continue two more statues to see **Cyril and Methodius,** the two

The Charles Bridge spans the Vltava River.

The cross is the Charles Bridge's oldest statue.

brothers who brought Christianity to this area around 865. Born in Thessaloniki (part of northern Greece today), Cyril and Methodius are credited with introducing Christianity not only to the Czechs, but to all Slavs; you'll see them revered from here to Dubrovnik, Warsaw, and Vladivostok. In this statue, they're bringing a pagan and primitive (bare-breasted) Czech woman into the Christian fold.

Now continue on, past the next statue, and find a small **brass relief** showing a cross with five stars embedded in the wall of the bridge (it's just below the little grate that sits on top of the stone banister). The relief depicts a figure floating in the river, with a semicircle of stars above him. This marks the traditional spot where the Czech patron saint John of Nepomuk is believed to have been tossed off the bridge and into the river.

For the rest of that story, continue past two more statue groups to the bronze Baroque statue of **St. John of Nepomuk,** with the five golden stars encircling his head. This statue always draws a crowd. John was a 14th-century priest to whom the queen confessed all her sins. According to a 17th-century legend, the king wanted to know his wife's secrets, but Father John dutifully refused to tell. The shiny plaque at the base of the statue shows what happened next: John was tortured and killed by being thrown off the bridge. The plaque shows the heave-ho. When he hit the water, five stars appeared, signifying his purity. Traditionally, people believe that touching the St. John plaque will make a wish come true.

Even if 19th-century Czechs defied their Catholic upbringing, they continued to be devoted to several patron saints who—even for agnostics—served as a rallying point for Czech national identity. For example, directly across from John is **St. Ludmila,** who raised her grandson to become St. Wenceslas—the 10th-century duke-turned-saint who first united the Czech people (and whose statue is found at the far end of the bridge).

▶ *A good way to end this walk is to enjoy the city and river view from near the center of the bridge. Stand here and survey your surroundings.*

⓳ View from Charles Bridge

First, look **upstream** (south). Notice the icebreakers immediately below. They protect the abutments upon which the bridge sits, as river ice has historically threatened its very survival. Look farther upstream for the tiny locks on the right side. While today's river traffic is limited to tourist boats, in earlier times timber, lashed like rafts, was floated down the river. On the left, farther upstream by the next bridge, is a building with a gilded crown atop its black dome. That's the National Theater. The rentable paddleboats plying the water are a romantic way to get a little exercise (see page 120).

Now, cross over and look **downstream.** Scan from right to left. You'll see the modern Four Seasons Hotel—that's the black roof, doing a pretty good job of fitting in. Farther down (with the green roof) is the large Neo-Renaissance concert hall of the Czech Philharmonic. Across the river and up the hill is a red needle of a giant metronome. It stands at the spot where a 50-foot-tall granite Joseph Stalin—flanked by eight equally tall workers and soldiers—stood from 1955 to 1962. To the right of Stalin's former perch (hiding under the trees and worth the climb on a hot summer day) is Prague's most popular beer garden.

Finally, capping the hill, follow the line of noble palaces that leads to the spire of the cathedral. It stands at the center of a castle, which—for a thousand years—has been the oversized seat of those who managed to impose their authority on the people living in the towns below.

And beneath your feet flows the majestic Vltava River—the watery thread that connects the Czech people.

▶ *From here, you can continue across the bridge to the Lesser Town (Kampa Island, on your left as you cross the bridge, is a tranquil spot to explore). You can also hike or take the tram up to the castle (a 10-minute walk to the right is the Malostranská stop for the Metro or for handy tram #22 or #23). Or retrace your steps across the bridge to enjoy more time in the Old Town.*

Jewish Quarter Tour

The fluctuating fortunes of Central Europe's Jews are etched in the streets of Prague's historic Jewish Quarter. This three-block area in the Old Town has been home to a Jewish community for a thousand years. The neighborhood features several impressive synagogues (including the oldest medieval one in Europe), an evocative cemetery, a powerful memorial honoring Czech Jews murdered in the Holocaust, and engaging exhibits on Jewish customs and tradition.

All but one of the sights are part of the **Jewish Museum in Prague** (Židovské Muzeum v Praze) and are treated as a single attraction. The remaining sight is the **Old-New Synagogue.** For me, this is the most interesting collection of Jewish sights in Europe, and—despite the high admission cost—well worth seeing.

Planning Your Time

You can see the sights in any order. My tour starts at the Maisel Synagogue, with interactive exhibits that give a good introduction to Jewish history in Bohemia. Next is the Jewish Quarter's most popular (and crowded) sight, the Pinkas Synagogue, a sobering reminder of Holocaust victims. This leads into the Old Jewish Cemetery, crowded with tombstones. The small Ceremonial Hall covers burial rites, and the Klausen Synagogue has an exposition on the cycle of Jewish holidays and the accompanying rituals. Break for coffee, then visit the Old-New Synagogue to soak up its majestic, medieval ambience. Finish with the ornately decorated Spanish Synagogue and its fine exhibits that bring Jewish history up to the moment.

Alternatively, you could plan your time around the crowded Pinkas Synagogue—be there right as it opens to avoid the crowds. Or, for a more leisurely option, start with the Old-New Synagogue, move on to the Klausen and Maisel, and then visit the Spanish Synagogue. Late in the day when the crowds have died down, finish with the powerful Pinkas.

ORIENTATION

Cost: You have three options: **Ticket #1** ("Jewish Town of Prague")—550 Kč, covers all six Jewish Museum sights plus the Old-New Synagogue; **Ticket #2**—400 Kč, covers Jewish Museum sights only; **Ticket #3**—220 Kč, covers the Old-New Synagogue only.

Hours: The six **Jewish Museum in Prague** sights are open Sun-Fri 9:00-18:00, Nov-March until 16:30, closed year-round on Sat and Jewish holidays; check the website for a complete list of holiday closures, especially if visiting in the fall. The **Old-New Synagogue** is open Sun-Thu 9:00-18:00, off-season until 17:00, Fri closes one hour before sunset, closed Sat and Jewish holidays.

Information: Jewish Museum in Prague, +420 222 317 191, www.jewishmuseum.cz; Old-New Synagogue, +420 222 317 191, www.synagogue.cz.

Buying Tickets and Avoiding Lines: Tickets are sold in person and on the Jewish Museum and Old-New Synagogue websites. In person, buy your ticket at the Maisel or Klausen synagogues or

Maisel Synagogue, with its excellent museum, is a good introduction to the Jewish Quarter.

at the Information Center at Maiselova 15 (near the intersection with Široká street). Avoid buying at the Pinkas Synagogue, which tends to have long lines.

The Pinkas Synagogue can be packed, especially between 10:00 and 11:30, so consider getting there right as it opens or later in the day.

Dress Code: Men are expected to cover their heads when entering an active synagogue or cemetery. It's respectful to bring a cap or borrow a museum-issued yarmulke.

Getting There: The Jewish Quarter is an easy walk from Old Town Square, up delightful Pařížská street (next to the green-domed Church of St. Nicholas). The Staroměstská Metro stop is just a couple blocks away.

Tours: The neighborhood is easy to see on your own using this chapter, and you'll find thoughtful information in English posted throughout the quarter. **Guided tours** are probably unnecessary (though I've listed one option—Wittmann Tours; see also my recommendations for local guides, some of whom specialize in Jewish Quarter tours; for details on both options, see the Activities chapter). The **audioguide** (300 Kč) is probably more information than you'll need.

Length of This Tour: Allow three hours (which can be split over several days—your ticket is good for a week). With limited time, focus on the Old-New Synagogue (for the ambience), the Pinkas Synagogue and Old Jewish Cemetery (for the history), and the Klausen Synagogue (for the exhibits).

Services: A café and WCs are at the ticket office at Maiselova 15. WCs are also at the exit from the cemetery and on the second floor of the Spanish Synagogue.

Nearby: The fine Museum of Medieval Art is only a few blocks from the Spanish Synagogue (see the Sights chapter).

Starring: The synagogues and cemetery of a faith and culture that has left its mark on Prague.

BACKGROUND

The Jewish people from the Holy Land (today's Israel and Palestine) were dispersed by the Romans nearly 2,000 years ago. Over the centuries, their culture survived in enclaves throughout the world; it was said that "the Torah was their sanctuary, which no army could destroy."

Jews first came to Prague in the 10th century. The least habitable, marshy area closest to the river bend was allotted to the Jewish community. The Jewish Quarter's main intersection (Maiselova and Široká streets) was the meeting point of two medieval trade routes. For centuries, Jews coexisted—at times tensely—with their non-Jewish Czech neighbors.

During the Crusades in the 12th century, the pope declared that Jews and Christians should not live together. Jews had to wear yellow badges, and their quarter was walled in and became a ghetto (minority neighborhood) of wooden houses and narrow lanes. In the 16th and 17th centuries, Prague had one of the biggest ghettos in Europe, with

The former Jewish ghetto now sports some of the city's toniest Art Nouveau facades.

The Synagogue

A synagogue is a place of public worship, where Jews gather to pray, sing, and read from the Torah. Most synagogues have similar features, though they vary depending on the congregation.

The synagogue generally faces toward Jerusalem (so in Prague, worshippers face east). At the east end is an alcove called the **ark,** which holds the Torah. These scriptures (the first five books of the Christian Old Testament) are written in Hebrew on scrolls wrapped in luxuriant cloth. The other main element of the synagogue is the **bema,** a platform from which the Torah is read aloud. In traditional Orthodox synagogues (like the Old-New and Pinkas synagogues), the bema is

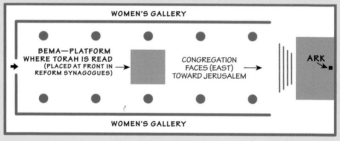

WOMEN'S GALLERY

BEMA—PLATFORM WHERE TORAH IS READ (PLACED AT FRONT IN REFORM SYNAGOGUES)

CONGREGATION FACES (EAST) TOWARD JERUSALEM

ARK

WOMEN'S GALLERY

11,000 inhabitants. Within its six gates, Prague's Jewish Quarter was a gaggle of 200 wooden buildings.

Faced with institutionalized bigotry and harassment, Jews relied mainly on profits from moneylending (forbidden to Christians) and community solidarity to survive. While their money bought them protection (the kings taxed Jewish communities heavily), it was often also a curse. Throughout Europe, when times got tough and Christian debts to the Jewish community mounted, entire Jewish communities were evicted or killed. The worst pogroms were in 1096 and in 1389, when around 3,000 Jews were killed.

In 1781, Emperor Josef II, motivated more by economic concerns than by religious freedom, eased much of the discrimination against Jews. In 1848, the Jewish Quarter's walls were torn down, and the neighborhood—named Josefov in honor of the emperor who provided

near the center of the hall, and the reader stands facing the same direction as the congregation. Other branches of Judaism place the bema at the front, and the reader faces the worshippers.

The synagogue walls might be decorated with elaborate patterns of vines or geometric designs, but never statues of people, as that might be seen as idol worship. A lamp above the ark is always kept lit, as it was in the ancient temple of Jerusalem, and candelabras called menorahs also recall the temple. Other common symbols are the two tablets of the Ten Commandments given to Moses, and the Star of David, representing the Jewish king's shield.

At a typical service, the congregation arrives at the start of Sabbath (Friday evening). As a sign of respect toward God, men don yarmulkes (small round caps). As the cantor leads songs and prayers, worshippers follow along in a book of weekly readings. At the heart of the service, everyone stands as the Torah is ceremoniously paraded, unwrapped, and placed on the bema. Someone—the rabbi, the cantor, or a congregant—reads the words aloud. The rabbi ("teacher") might give a commentary on the Torah passage.

Services similar to this have gone on in Prague's Jewish Quarter for a thousand years.

this small measure of tolerance—was incorporated as a district of the Old Town.

In 1897, ramshackle Josefov was razed and replaced by a new modern town—the original 31 streets and 220 buildings became 10 streets and 83 buildings. They leveled the medieval-era buildings (except the synagogues) and turned this into perhaps Europe's finest Art Nouveau neighborhood. Here (and all along this walk) you'll enjoy stately facades with gables, turrets, elegant balconies, mosaics, statues, and all manner of architectural marvels. By the 1930s, Prague's Jewish community was prospering.

But then World War II hit. Of the 55,000 Jews living in Prague in 1939, just 10,000 survived the Holocaust to see liberation in 1945. And in the communist era—when the atheistic regime was also anti-Semitic—recovery was slow.

Today Prague's Jewish community numbers about 7,000 people. A community school run by the Lauder Foundation is popular among Jews and non-Jews alike. And while today's modern grid plan has replaced the higgledy-piggledy medieval streets of old, Široká ("Wide Street") remains the main street. A few Jewish-themed shops and restaurants in the area add extra ambience to this (otherwise modern) neighborhood.

THE TOUR BEGINS

▶ *The center of the neighborhood is the intersection of Maiselova and Široká streets. A half-block south on Maiselova street is the...*

❶ Maisel Synagogue (Maiselova Synagóga)

This synagogue was built as a private place of worship for the Maisel family during the late 16th century. This was a "golden age" for Prague's Jews, when Habsburg rulers lifted the many bans and persecutions against them. Maisel, the wealthy financier of the Habsburg king, lavished his riches on this synagogue.

Before entering, notice the facade featuring the Ten Commandments top and center (standard in synagogues). Below that is the symbol for Prague's Jewish community: the Star of David, with the pointed hat local Jews wore here through medieval times.

Inside, the interactive exhibit retraces a thousand years of Jewish history in Bohemia and Moravia. Well explained in English, topics include the origin of the Star of David, Jewish mysticism, the golem legend, the history of discrimination, and the creation of Prague's ghetto. Pre-WWII photographs of small-town synagogues from the region

Pinkas Synagogue lists Holocaust victims.

Displays about Jewish culture at Maisel

Prague's Jewish Quarter

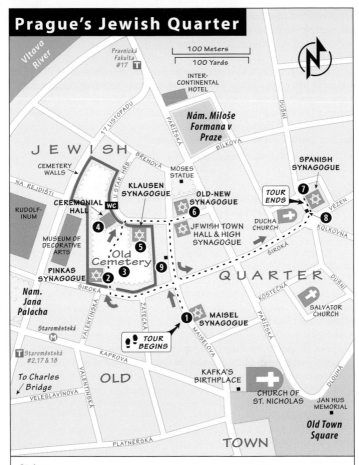

100 Meters

100 Yards

Vltava River

Pravnická Fakulta #17

INTER-CONTINENTAL HOTEL

Nám. Miloše Formana v Praze

J E W I S H

CEMETERY WALLS

MOSES STATUE

KLAUSEN SYNAGOGUE

OLD-NEW SYNAGOGUE

SPANISH SYNAGOGUE

TOUR ENDS

NA REJDIŠTI

CEREMONIAL HALL

WC

RUDOLF-INUM

MUSEUM OF DECORATIVE ARTS

Old Cemetery

JEWISH TOWN HALL & HIGH SYNAGOGUE

DUCHA CHURCH

PINKAS SYNAGOGUE

Nam. Jana Palacha

ŠIROKÁ

ŠIROKÁ

Q U A R T E R

KOSTEČNÁ

SALVATOR CHURCH

Staroměstská

Staroměstská #2,17 & 18

To Charles Bridge

VELESLAVÍNOVA

KAPROVA

O L D

MAISEL SYNAGOGUE

TOUR BEGINS

KAFKA'S BIRTHPLACE

CHURCH OF ST. NICHOLAS

JAN HUS MEMORIAL

Old Town Square

PLATNÉŘSKÁ

T O W N

Sights

1 Maisel Synagogue
2 Pinkas Synagogue
3 Old Jewish Cemetery
4 Ceremonial Hall
5 Klausen Synagogue
6 Old-New Synagogue
7 Spanish Synagogue

Other

8 Kafka Statue
9 Info/Ticket Office

are projected on a large screen. Notice the eastern wall, with the holy ark containing a precious Torah mantel. A bird's-eye-view video takes you through the streets of the ghetto as they appear in a 1787 model of Prague.

In World War II, this synagogue became a warehouse for Jewish artifacts after the Nazis ordered synagogues to send their riches—Torah scrolls, books, menorahs—to Prague to be catalogued and filed away in the closed-down Jewish museum. The communists reopened the museum but made sure these objects were displayed with little attention to their historical or ritual context.

▶ *Walk to Široká street and turn left—following the cemetery wall—to find the...*

❷ Pinkas Synagogue (Pinkasova Synagóga)

A site of Jewish worship since the 16th century, this synagogue is certainly historic. But these days it's best known as a poignant memorial to the victims of the Nazis.

Enter and go down the steps leading to the **main hall** of this small late-Gothic/early-Renaissance synagogue. Aaron Meshulam Horowitz, a prosperous merchant and man of influence in his day, built the synagogue in 1535. Notice the old stone-and-wrought-iron bema in the middle, the niche for the ark at the far end, the crisscross vaulting overhead, and the Art Nouveau stained glass filling the place with light.

But the focus of this synagogue is its walls, inscribed with the handwritten **names** of 77,297 Czech Jews sent to the gas chambers at Auschwitz and other camps. Czech Jews were especially hard hit by the Holocaust. More than 155,000 of them passed through the nearby Terezín camp alone. Most died with no grave marker, but they are remembered here.

The names are carefully organized: Family names are in red, followed in black by the individual's first name, birthday, and date of death (if known) or date of deportation. You can tell by the dates that families often perished together.

The names are gathered in groups by hometowns (listed in gold, as well as on placards at the base of the wall). Prague's dead fill the main hall. On the ark wall is a list of the ghettos and extermination camps that received Czech Jews—Terezín, as well as Dachau, Bergen-Belsen,

The Pinkas Synagogue's Gothic main hall has the platform from which the Torah is read.

and the notorious Oświęcim (Auschwitz). As you ponder this sad sight, you'll hear the somber reading of the names alternating with a cantor singing the Psalms.

Among the names are the grandparents of (Prague-born) former US Secretary of State Madeleine Albright—Arnošt and Olga Korbel, listed at the far end of the long wall.

Climb eight steps into the **women's gallery,** where (as is typical in traditional synagogues) the women worshipped separately from the men. On the left wall, upper part, find some names in poor condition. These are originals, and some of the oldest. The name project began in the 1950s. But the communist regime closed the synagogue and erased virtually everything. With freedom, in 1989, the Pinkas Synagogue was reopened and many names had to be rewritten.

On your way out, watch on the right for the easy-to-miss stairs up to the small **Terezín Children's Art Exhibit.** Well described in English, these drawings were made by Jewish children imprisoned at Terezín, 40 miles northwest of Prague (a worthy day trip from here). This is where the Nazis shipped Prague's Jews for processing before transporting them east to death camps. Thirty-five thousand Jews died at Terezín, and many tens of thousands more died in other camps.

Of the 8,000 children transported from Terezín, only 240 came back. The teacher who led the drawing lessons and hid these artworks believed children could use imagination to liberate their minds from the camp. Their art survives to defy fate. The collection is organized into poignant themes: dreams of returning to Prague, yearning for a fantasized Holy Land, memories of the simple times before imprisonment, biblical and folkloric tales focusing on the themes of good and evil, and scenes of everyday life at Terezín.

▶ *Exiting the Pinkas Synagogue, the visit leads up several stairs into the adjoining cemetery.*

❸ Old Jewish Cemetery (Starý Židovský Hřbitov)

Enter one of the most wistful scenes in Europe—Prague's Old Jewish Cemetery—and meander along a path through 12,000 evocative tombstones. They're old, eroded, inscribed in Hebrew, and leaning this way and that. A few of the dead have larger ark-shaped tombs. Most have a simple epitaph with the name, date, and a few of the deceased's virtues. Among the dead buried here are Aaron Meshulam Horowitz

The Old Jewish Cemetery, once the only place Prague's Jews could be buried

(builder of the Pinkas Synagogue), Mordechai Maisel (of the Maisel Synagogue), and Rabbi Loew (of golem fame; see "From Golems to Robots" sidebar, later).

From 1439 until 1787, this was the only burial ground allowed for the Jews of Prague. Over time, the bodies had to be stacked on top of each other—seven or eight deep—so the number of people buried here is actually closer to 85,000. Graves were never relocated because of the Jewish belief that, once buried, a body should not be moved. Layer by layer, the cemetery grew into a small plateau. And as things settled over time, the tombstones became crooked. Tune in to the noise of passing cars outside, and you realize that you're several feet above the modern street level—which is already high above the medieval level.

People place pebbles on honored tombstones. This custom, a sign of respect, shows that the dead have not been forgotten and recalls the old days, when rocks were placed upon a sandy gravesite to keep the body covered. Others leave scraps of paper that contain prayers and wishes. The most popular tombstone on which to place pebbles, coins, and paper is the reddish tomb found alongside the wall (the path leads right by it). This is the burial site of Prague's beloved Rabbi Loew. The cemetery is called Beth Chaim in Hebrew, meaning "House of Life."

▶ *The cemetery visit spills out at the far end, right at the entrances to the Ceremonial Hall (on your left) and Klausen Synagogue (right).*

❹ Ceremonial Hall (Obřadní Síň)

This rustic stone tower (1911) was a mortuary house used to prepare the body and perform purification rituals before burial. The inside is painted in fanciful, flowery Neo-Romanesque style. It's filled with a worthwhile exhibition on Jewish medicine, death, and burial traditions. A series of crude but instructive paintings (c. 1780, hanging on walls throughout the house) show how the "burial brotherhood" took care of the ill and buried the dead. As all are equal before God, the rich and poor alike were buried in embroidered linen shrouds similar to the one you'll see on display.

▶ *Next door is the...*

❺ Klausen Synagogue (Klauzová Synagóga)

The 17th-century Baroque-style synagogue is impressive and historic—again, locate the bema, the ark, and the women's gallery above—but the focus here is the displays on Jewish religious practices.

Ground-floor displays touch on Jewish holidays. The bema displays a Torah (the first five books of the Christian Old Testament) and the solid silver pointers used when reading it—necessary because the Torah is not to be touched. Now start at the entrance and work clockwise. In the first big, horizontal display case, the biggest book is a Torah (1444) associated with the great medieval philosopher Maimonides. The second display case has shofar horns, blown ritually during Jewish high holy days. Up in the elevated area, the ark contains elaborately wrapped Torah scrolls ornamented with silver. In the next cases you'll see a seder plate, used to serve the six traditional foods of Passover; a tiny "Omer Calendar," an ingenious device used to keep track of the holidays; and a palm frond *(lulav),* waved when reciting a blessing during the holiday of Sukkot. At the back of the synagogue are objects from the Prague community, including menorahs used in both synagogues and the Hanukkah celebration.

Upstairs, exhibits illustrate the rituals of everyday Jewish life. It starts at birth. There are good-luck amulets to ensure a healthy baby, and a wooden cradle that announces, "This little one will become big." A male baby is circumcised (see the knife). The baby grows to celebrate

Klausen Synagogue, with its women's gallery (left), ark for Torah scrolls (far end), and displays

a coming-of-age Bar or Bat Mitzvah around age 12 or 13. Marriage takes place under a canopy, and the couple sets up their home—the exhibit ends with some typical furnishings.

▶ *Exiting the synagogue, turn right and go one block down to the...*

❻ Old-New Synagogue (Staronová Synagóga, a.k.a. Altneuschul)

For more than 700 years, this has been the most important synagogue and the central building in Josefov. Built in 1270, it's the oldest synagogue in Central Europe (and some say the oldest still-working synagogue in all of Europe). A prosaic explanation derives the name from the fact that it was "New" when built but became "Old" when other, newer synagogues came on the scene. The building's exterior is simple, with a unique sawtooth gable. Standing like a reinforced bunker, it feels as though it has survived plenty of hard times.

As you enter, you descend a few steps below street level to 13th-century street level and the medieval world.

The **interior** is pure Gothic—thick pillars, soaring arches, and narrow lancet windows. If it looks like a church, well, the architects were Christians. The stonework is original, and the woodwork (the paneling and benches) is also old. This was one of the first Gothic buildings in Prague.

Seven centuries later, it's still a working synagogue. There's the stone bema in the middle where the Torah is read aloud, and the ark at the far end, where the sacred scrolls are kept. To the right of the ark, one chair is bigger, with a Star of David above it. This chair always remains empty out of respect for great rabbis of the past. Where's the women's gallery? Here, women worshipped in rooms that flanked the

The Old-New Synagogue may be Europe's oldest.   Its interior still looks medieval.

From Golems to Robots

One of Prague's most popular 19th-century legends is associated with the Old-New Synagogue. Around 1600, Rabbi Loew (who was indeed a real person) wanted to protect Prague's Jews from persecution. So he created a creature out of Vltava River clay, known as the golem. He placed a stone in the golem's forehead (or, some say, under his tongue), bringing the beast to life.

The golem guarded the ghetto, but—in keeping with the Jewish custom of reserving the Sabbath as the day of rest—Rabbi Loew always removed the life-giving stone on Friday night. But one day he forgot, the golem went on a rampage, and Rabbi Loew had to remove the stone for good. He hid the golem in the attic of the Old-New Synagogue, where it's said to be to this day. The attic is closed to tourists, but you can circle around behind the building to see an iron-rung ladder that leads to the still-dangerous lair of the golem. Meanwhile, believers in such legends remain convinced that the stone can still be found somewhere in the streets of Prague—keep an eye out.

The story of the golem inspired the early-20th-century Czech writer Karel Čapek to write his play *R.U.R.*, about artificially created beings who eventually turn on their creators. To describe the creatures, he coined the Czech word *roboti,* "indentured workers," which was quickly absorbed into English as "robot."

hall, watching the service through those horizontal windows in the walls.

The big red banner rising above the bema is (a copy of) a gift from Charles IV, given in honor of the Jewish community's service to the crown. For centuries it has been proudly carried by the Jewish community during parades. On the banner is a Star of David and the Hebrew prayer at the heart of the service: "Hear, O Israel..." Within the Star of David is pictured the yellow-pointed hat that Jewish men were obliged to wear.

Twelve is a popular number in the decor, because it symbolizes the 12 tribes of Israel: There are 12 windows, 12 vines in the frieze at the base of the bema, 12 bunches of grapes carved over the entrance, and so on. While Nazis routinely destroyed synagogues, this most historic synagogue in the country survived because the Nazis intended it to be part of their "Museum of the Extinct Jewish Race."

Jews were not permitted in the Stonemasons Guild, but it's nonetheless taken as a sign of how well Prague's Jews were doing that guild members built this Jewish place of worship. Notice that they outfitted the ceiling with clumsy five-ribbed vaulting. The builders were good at four-ribbed vaulting, but it wasn't right for a synagogue, because it resulted in a cross.

Before leaving, check out the **lobby** (the long hall where you show your ticket). It has two fortified old lockers in which the most heavily taxed community in medieval Prague stored its money in anticipation of the taxman's arrival.

▸ *The Spanish Synagogue is four blocks from here. Before moving on, check out the dynamic statue of a kneeling man in the adjacent park: This is Moses in the act of inscribing the name of Adam on parchment, symbolizing the start of the human journey.*

Head up Maiselova street (toward Old Town Square), and turn left on Široká, which leads to the...

❼ Spanish Synagogue (Španělská Synagóga)

In its size and ornateness, this building is typical of many synagogues built around Central Europe in the late 1800s. With the reforms accompanying the transformation of the Austro-Hungarian Empire in 1867, Jews were finally granted full rights. To express their new self-confidence, Jews built in a deliberately distinct style that evoked their golden days in Muslim-ruled Spain. It has been recently renovated, so be aware that some details may have changed from what's described here.

Before entering, circle around the left side of the building for a better view of the **facade.** It's called "Spanish," but the style is really Moorish: horseshoe arches atop slender columns, different colored stone, elaborate tracery, and topped with pseudo-minarets. Though the building is relatively new, it stands on the site of Prague's oldest synagogue (from c. 1150), which burned down during the pogrom of 1389.

The Spanish Synagogue's Moorish design refers to the Jews' golden period in Muslim-ruled Spain.

Inside, the decor is exotic and awe-inspiring. Intricate inter-weaving designs of stars and vines cover every inch of the red-gold and green walls and ceiling. A rose window with a stylized Star of David graces the ark.

The new synagogue housed a new movement within Judaism—a Reform congregation—that worshipped in a more modern way. The bema has been moved to the front of the synagogue, so the officiant faces the congregation. There's also a prominent organ (upper right) to accompany the singing.

Displays of Jewish history bring us through the 18th, 19th, and tumultuous 20th centuries to today. In the 1800s, Jews were increasingly accepted and successful in the greater society. But tolerance brought a dilemma—was it better to assimilate within the dominant culture or to join the growing Zionist homeland movement? To reform the religion or to remain orthodox?

Upstairs, the **balcony exhibits** focus on Czech Jews in the 1900s. Start in the area near the organ, which explains the modern era of Jewish Prague, including the late-19th-century development of Josefov. Then work your way around the balcony, with exhibits on Jewish writers (Franz Kafka), philosophers (Edmund Husserl), and other notables (Freud). This intellectual renaissance came to an abrupt halt with World War II and the mass deportations to Terezín (see more sad displays on life there, including more children's art and a box full of tefillin prayer cases). The final displays bring it home: After 2,000 years of living away from their Holy Land roots, the Jewish people had a homeland—the modern nation of Israel. Finish your visit across the landing in the **Winter Synagogue,** showing a trove of silver—Kiddush cups, Hanukkah lamps, Sabbath candlesticks, and Torah ornaments. This collection got its start in the early 20th century, when the Jewish Museum was formed, and began its important work of preserving places and artifacts that otherwise might have been forever lost.

▶ *Next to the Spanish Synagogue is a bizarre ❽ **statue** by Jaroslav Róna commemorating the writer **Franz Kafka.** It's a reference to a short story by Kafka ("Description of a Struggle") in which the oppressed protagonist is carried through an imaginary landscape on the shoulders of a headless giant, which supposedly represents his other, dominant self.*

Our walk is over. You've explored the history of one of countless Jewish communities in Europe with an important story to tell.

Wenceslas Square Walk

Václavské Náměstí

Though the Old Town gets all the attention (and most of the tourists), the New Town—and particularly its main square—is more the people's Prague. In the 14th century, the king created this new town, tripling the size of what would become Prague. This short walk focuses on the New Town's centerpiece, Wenceslas Square—once the horse market of this busy working-class district. Along the way, we'll see sights associated with the square's great moments in history, including the watershed protests of 1989 that helped create the modern nation.

ORIENTATION

Length of This Walk: Allow an hour (add more time if dropping into sights along the way).

When to Go: This walk can be done at any time—and may work particularly well in the evening, after other sights have closed. However, if interested in visiting the Cold War Museum, plan your walk around their tour times.

National Museum: 250 Kč, daily 10:00-18:00, most Wednesdays opens at 9:00; Václavské Náměstí 68.

Cold War Museum: 400 Kč for one-hour guided tour; English tours daily at 11:00, 13:00, 14:30, and 16:00 from inside the Jalta Hotel; www.en.muzeum-studene-valky.cz.

Getting There: The walk starts at the top of Wenceslas Square, in front of the National Museum; the nearest Metro stop is called Muzeum. If you're coming from the Old Town, hike the length of the square up to the top to start the walk.

Eating: This walk passes a popular ice-cream parlor. Dozens of other eateries are nearby (see my recommendations on page 155).

Starring: Urban bustle, a secluded garden, and a thousand years of Czech history—from St. Václav to Václav Havel.

THE WALK BEGINS

▶ *At the top of Wenceslas Square, stand under the huge statue of "Good King Wenceslas" on a horse.*

Join Wenceslas as he gazes proudly down this long, broad square. It's actually more like a boulevard busy with cars, with a parklike median right down the middle. It's a huge expanse, covering more than 10 acres. Stand here and take in the essence of modern Prague.

Think of how this place has served as a kind of national stage for important events in the history of the Czech people. In 1918, it was here that jubilant crowds gathered to celebrate the end of World War I and the subsequent creation of modern Czechoslovakia. During World War II, this was the scene of Nazi occupation, and then of rioting Czechs who drove the Nazis out. In the spring of 1968, the Czechs gathered here to protest against their next set of oppressors, the communist Soviets. These "Prague Spring" reforms gained international

View down Wenceslas Square, covering 10 acres   Wenceslas Square, for both cars and people

attention, but eventually Soviet tanks rumbled into town and crushed the rebellion. Then, in 1989, more than 300,000 Czechs and Slovaks converged right here to reclaim their freedom once again.

Which brings us to today. Survey the square for a snapshot of "the now." You'll see businesspeople, families, dumpster divers, security guards, hipsters, and students. It sums up the changes and rapid transformation of society here over the past 100 years.

▶ *But let's go back to the very beginning. Turn your attention now to the big equestrian statue of...*

❶ Duke Wenceslas I

The "Good King" of Christmas-carol fame was actually a wise and benevolent 10th-century duke. Václav (as he's called by locals) united the Czech people, back when this land was known as Bohemia. A rare example of a well-educated and literate ruler, Wenceslas Christianized and lifted the culture. He astutely allied the powerless Czechs with the Holy Roman Empire of the German nation (making him likewise revered in the German-speaking world). And he began to fortify Prague's castle as a center of Czech government. After his murder in 929, Wenceslas was canonized as a saint. He became a symbol of Czech nationalism (and appears on the 20 Kč coin). Later kings knelt before his tomb to be crowned. And he remains an icon of Czech unity whenever the nation has to rally. Like King Arthur in England, Wenceslas is more legend than history, but he symbolizes the country's birth.

The statue is surrounded by the four other Czech patron saints. Notice the focus on books. A small nation without great military power, the Czechs have thinkers as national heroes, not warriors.

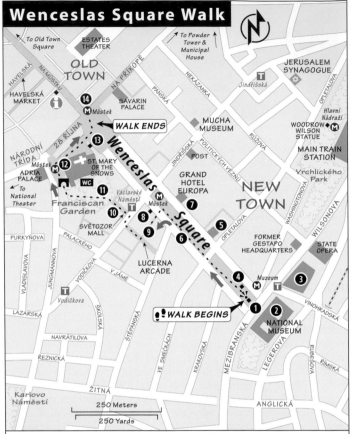

Wenceslas Square Walk

1. Duke Wenceslas I Statue
2. National Museum
3. Communist-Era Building
4. Memorial to the Victims of 1969
5. Jalta Hotel & Cold War Museum
6. Walking down Wenceslas Square
7. Grand Hotel Europa
8. Velvet Revolution Balcony
9. Lucerna Arcade
10. Světozor Mall
11. Franciscan Garden
12. Jungmann Square
13. Baťa Shoe Store
14. Můstek & Old City Wall

▶ *Circle behind the statue and stand beneath the tail; turn your attention to the impressive building at the top of Wenceslas Square.*

❷ National Museum

This grand, lavishly restored building dates from the 19th century, when modern nation-states were forming in Europe and the Czech people were still living under the auspices of Austria's Habsburg Empire. Bold structures like this Neo-Renaissance building were a way to show the world that the Czech lands had a distinct culture and a heritage of precious artifacts, and that Czechs deserved their own nation.

Look closely at the columns on the building's facade. Those light-colored patches (meticulously preserved during the latest renovation) are covering holes where Soviet bullets hit during the 1968 crackdown. The state-of-the-art interior is filled with diverse exhibits ranging from minerals to modern history.

▶ *To the left of the National Museum (as you face it) is a...*

❸ Communist-Era Building

This out-of-place modern structure (combining a 1930s core with a 1960s shell) once housed the rubber-stamp Czechoslovak Parliament back when it voted in lockstep with Moscow. At its base, under the canopy, is a statue from those days, in the style known as Socialist Realism. As was typical, it shows not just a worker...but a *triumphant* worker.

Between 1994 and 2008, this building was home to Radio Free Europe. After communism fell, RFE lost some of its funding and could no longer afford its Munich headquarters. In gratitude for its

A lavish symbol of 19th-century nationalism

A blocky symbol of 20th-century communism

broadcasts—which had kept Eastern Europe in touch with real news—the Czech government offered this building to RFE for 1 Kč a year. But as RFE energetically beamed its American message deep into the Muslim world from here, it drew attention—and threats—from Al-Qaeda. In 2009, RFE moved to a new fortress-like headquarters literally across the cemetery wall from Franz Kafka's grave. Now this is an annex of the National Museum that displays temporary exhibits.

The communist authorities also built the nearby Muzeum Metro stop and the busy highway that runs between the top of the square and the National Museum. Since the communists checked out, city leaders have struggled with the legacy of this heavy-handed infrastructure, which makes the museum area the most polluted spot in the city.

Along the busy street just past the communist-era building (hard to see from here) is the **State Opera,** which was built in the 1880s as the New German Theater—at a time when Prague's once-dominant German population was feeling neglected after the opening of the Czechs' National Theater. Across the road is a cold, Neoclassical building that was the local Gestapo headquarters during Nazi times. This chilling juxtaposition of high culture with authoritarian control pretty much sums up the Czechs' love/hate relationship with their powerful German and Austrian neighbors.

▶ *Start walking down Wenceslas Square. Pause about 30 yards along, at the little patch of bushes. In the ground on the downhill side of those bushes is a...*

❹ Memorial to the Victims of 1969

After the Russian crackdown of 1968, a young philosophy student named Jan Palach, inspired by monks immolating themselves in protest in Vietnam, decided that the best way to stoke the flame of independence was to do the same right here. On January 16, 1969, Palach stood on the steps of the National Museum and ignited his body. He died a few days later. Hundreds of thousands turned up for his funeral, as his act resonated with the dark and desperate mood of the occupied country. A month later, another student did the same thing, followed by another. Czechs are keen on anniversaries, and 20 years after Palach's defining act, in 1989, hundreds of Czechs gathered here again in protest. A sense of new possibility swept through the city, and 10 months later, the communists were history.

▶ *Farther down the square, locate the building on the right with the beige travertine facade (and many balconies). This is the…*

❺ Jalta Hotel and Cold War Museum

This building is most representative of the 1950s Neoclassical, Socialist Realist style. Designed at the height of the Cold War as a hotel for VIPs, it came with an underground crisis-fallout shelter that visiting Soviet generals could use as a command center in case nuclear war broke out. The bunkers were refurbished back to their original state by a group of Czechoslovak army fans and converted into the ▲ Cold War Museum (visits by tour only; for details, see the Sights chapter).

▶ *Continue down Wenceslas Square.*

❻ Walking down Wenceslas Square

Wenceslas Square is part of Prague's New Town, one of the four traditional quarters. Prague got its start in the ninth century at the castle. It spilled across the river to the Old Town, which was fortified with a city wall. By the 1300s, the Old Town was bursting at the seams. King Charles IV expanded the town outward, tripling the size of Prague. Wenceslas Square, a central feature of the New Town, was originally founded as a horse market.

As you walk, notice the architecture. Unlike the historic Old Town, nearly everything here is from the past two centuries. Wenceslas Square is a showcase of Prague's many architectural styles: You'll see Neo-Gothic, Neo-Renaissance, and Neo-Baroque from the 19th century. There's curvaceous Art Nouveau from around 1900. And there's the modernist response to Art Nouveau—Functionalism from the mid-20th century, where the watchword was "form follows function" and beauty took a back seat to practicality. You'll see buildings from the 1950s communist era, forgettable glass-and-steel buildings of the 1970s, and modern stores from the 2000s.

On the right-hand side of Wenceslas Square is ❼ **Grand Hotel Europa.** It's the one with the dazzling yellow Art Nouveau exterior. If you're a fan of Art Nouveau, you'll want to check out Prague's Mucha Museum (just up the street behind this hotel and described in the 📖 Mucha Museum Tour chapter).

Opposite Grand Hotel Europa (on the left side of the square), find the Marks & Spencer building and its **balcony** (partly obscured by trees).

▶ *Standing here in the center of Wenceslas Square, look up at that balcony and take a moment to consider the events of November 1989.*

❽ The Velvet Revolution

Picture the scene on this square on a cold November night in 1989. Czechoslovakia had been oppressed for the previous 40 years by the communist Soviet Union. But now the Soviet empire was beginning to crumble, jubilant Germans were dancing on top of the shattered Berlin Wall, and the Czechs were getting a whiff of freedom.

Czechoslovakia's revolution began with a bunch of teenagers, who—following a sanctioned gathering—decided to march on Wenceslas Square. They were surrounded and beaten by the communist riot police, and days later their enraged parents, friends, and other members of the community poured into this square to protest. Night after night, this huge square was filled with more than 300,000 ecstatic Czechs and Slovaks who believed freedom was at hand. Each night they would jingle their key chains in the air as if saying to their communist leaders, "It's time for you to go home now." Finally, they gathered and found that their communist overlords had left—and freedom was theirs.

On that night, as thousands filled this square, a host of famous people appeared on that balcony to greet the crowd. There was a well-known priest and a rock star famous for his rebellion against authority. There was Alexander Dubček, the hero of the Prague Spring reforms of 1968. And there was Václav Havel, the charismatic playwright who had spent years in prison, becoming a symbol of resistance—a kind of

One of Europe's best Art Nouveau facades

Memorial to the Velvet Revolution

Czech Nelson Mandela. Now he was free. Havel's voice boomed over the gathered masses. He proclaimed the resignation of the Politburo and the imminent freedom of the Republic of Czechoslovakia. He pulled out a ring of keys and jingled it. Thousands of keys jingled back in response to indicate time was up.

In previous years, the communist authorities would have sent in tanks to crush the impudent masses. But by 1989, the Soviet empire was collapsing and the Czech government was shaky. Locals think that Soviet head of state Mikhail Gorbachev (mindful of the Tiananmen Square massacre in China a few months before) might have made a phone call recommending a nonviolent response. Whatever happened, the communist regime was overthrown with hardly any blood being spilled. It was achieved through sheer people power—thanks to the masses of defiant Czechs who gathered here peacefully in Wenceslas Square, and Slovaks doing the same in Bratislava. A British journalist called it "The Velvet Revolution," and the name caught on in the West. Locals call it simply "The Revolution."

▶ *Look downhill to the bottom of Wenceslas Square. We'll be heading there eventually. But we'll take a less-touristed detour to the left, with some interesting things to see.*

Opposite Grand Hotel Europa is a shopping mall called the Lucerna Arcade. Use the entry marked Pasáž Rokoko *and walk in. Continue about 100 yards straight through the mall until you find a horse hanging from the ceiling.*

❾ Lucerna Arcade

This grand mall retains some of its Art Deco glamour from the 1930s. But that's not its most notable feature. In the middle of it all, you'll see a sculpture—called ***Wenceslas Riding an Upside-Down Horse***—hanging like a swing from a glass dome. David Černý, who created the statue in 1999, is one of the Czech Republic's most original contemporary artists. Always aspiring to provoke controversy, Černý has painted a menacing Russian tank pink, attached crawling babies to the rocket-like Žižkov TV tower, hung Sigmund Freud on an iron rod, and sunk a shark-like Saddam Hussein inside an aquarium.

The grand staircase leading up from beneath the suspended sculpture takes you to a lavish 1930s Prague **cinema,** which shows mostly art-house films in their original language with Czech subtitles.

A modern artist's take on King Wenceslas in the Lucerna Arcade, a great place to just hang

The same staircase leads up to the swanky, Art Deco **Café Lucerna,** with windows overlooking this atrium. And in the basement, there's the popular **Lucerna Music Bar,** which hosts '80s and '90s video parties on weekends, and concerts on other nights (for details, see the Activities chapter).

▶ *From the horse, turn right and head for the side exit (passing the entrance to the Lucerna Music Bar on your left). After you exit into the open air, jog a bit to the right across busy Vodičkova street (with a handy tram stop), where you'll find the entrance to the Světozor Mall— it's a few steps to the right, by the* Kino Světozor *sign. Go on in.*

⑩ Světozor Mall

As you enter the mall, look up at a glass window from the 1930s advertising Tesla, a now-defunct Czech radio manufacturer. The window lends a retro brightness to the place. On the left, pause at the always-busy Ovocný Světozor ("World of Fruit"), a popular franchise ice-cream joint (their specialty is banana-strawberry). They also sell cakes, milkshakes, and "little breads"—delightful Czech-style open-face sandwiches—really cheap. English menus are available on request. While licking your cone, ponder this: This nondescript space once housed the Theatre of the Seven Small Forms (known as the Semafor Theater), the center of the unprecedented creative outburst of the Czech culture that culminated in what became known as the Prague Spring.

▶ *Walk under the* Tesla *sign to leave the mall. As you exit, turn left immediately to enter the gates of the peaceful...*

Art Deco remnant in the Světozor Mall

Franciscan Garden, a New Town oasis

⓫ Franciscan Garden

Ahhh! This garden's white benches and spreading rosebushes are a universe away from the fast beat of the city, which throbs behind the buildings corralling this little oasis.

The peacefulness reflects the purpose of its Franciscan origin. St. Francis, the founder of the order, thought God's presence could be found in nature. In the 1600s, Prague became an important center for a group of Franciscans from Ireland. Enjoy the herb garden and children's playground. (A WC is just out the far side of the garden.) The park is a popular place for a discreet rendezvous; it's famous among locals for kicking off romances.

Looming up at the far end of the garden is a tall, truncated building that looks like it's been chopped in half. When the New Town was founded, its leaders commissioned **St. Mary of the Snows Church**—with its elegant white Gothic walls and lofty apse—to rival St. Vitus Cathedral, across the river. Like St. Vitus, construction halted with the religious wars of the 1400s; unlike St. Vitus, it never resumed. (If you want to peek inside, we'll pass the entrance soon.)

▶ *Exit the garden at the opposite corner from where you entered (past the little yellow gardening pavilion, which now houses a design boutique, and the herb garden). You'll pass a handy pay WC, then pop out through a big gate into...*

⓬ Jungmann Square (Jungmannovo Náměstí)

The statue depicts **Josef Jungmann** (1773-1847), who revived the Czech language at a time when it was considered a simple peasants' tongue. To the left as you face Jungmann is the decadent, almost overly ornamented Adria Palace—which served as Václav Havel's "base camp" during those electrifying two weeks in November of 1989.

Turn right past the statue and follow the black paving stones as they cut through the skinny square. Ahead and on the right, look for the ⓭ **Baťa shoe store,** one of the big entrepreneurial success stories of prewar Czechoslovakia. By making affordable but good-quality shoes, Tomáš Baťa's company thrived through the Depression years, only to be seized by the communists after World War II. The family moved their operation abroad but have now reopened their factory in their hometown of Zlín. Today, Baťa shoes remain popular with Czechs—and international fashionistas.

Just to the right of the shoe store, near the corner of the square, notice the zigzag **Cubist lamppost**—one of many such flourishes scattered around this city, from the brief period when this experimental, uniquely Czech style was in vogue. Just beyond the lamppost is a hidden beer garden that huddles around the base of the church.

▶ *Keep following those black paving stones through the glassed-in gallery next to the Baťa shoe store. You'll emerge near the bottom of Wenceslas Square.*

⓮ Můstek and the Old City Wall

The bottom of the square marks the border between the Old Town and New Town. You'll notice the Metro stop Můstek, meaning "Bridge." You used to have to cross a bridge here, then pass through a fortified gate, to enter the Old Town, which was surrounded by a protective wall and moat. (In the Můstek Metro station you can see the original Old Town gate in the wall.) The Old Town and New Town were officially merged in 1784.

Let's finish the walk by bringing Czech history up to the moment. The Soviets were tossed out in the 1989 Velvet Revolution. Then the Czech Republic and Slovakia peacefully separated in 1993. Through the 1990s, the fledgling Czech Republic was guided by President Václav Havel, that former key-jingling playwright. In 2004, the Czech Republic became a member of the European Union. Today, the Czech people are experiencing economic challenges, including inflation and higher energy costs, but the overall economy is stable. The Czech Republic finds its traditional political parties in crisis—much like others worldwide—with centrist populists as well as left and right extremists gaining appeal. The history of the Czech people continues to be written. In the meantime, their capital, Prague, remains one of the most popular tourist destinations in Europe.

▶ *Our walk is done. Here at Můstek, you have many options: Continue straight ahead into the Old Town; turn right along Na Příkopě street (the former moat) to visit the Mucha Museum, Municipal House, or Museum of Communism; or go left along Národní street to the National Theater and the river. For places farther afield, you can hop on the Metro at Můstek. The rest of Prague is yours to enjoy.*

Mucha Museum Tour

Muchovo Museum

Famous in his time but woefully underappreciated outside his homeland today (with the exception of Japan), Alphonse Mucha (1860-1939) was an enormously talented Czech artist who wowed the art world as he harnessed and developed the emerging style of Art Nouveau.

Mucha's slinky theater posters—which graced the streets of Paris at the turn of the century—earned him international fame. He could have done anything, but he chose to return to his home country and use his talent to celebrate Czech culture. This small but endearingly earnest museum is a great place to appreciate Mucha's artistic genius.

ORIENTATION

Cost and Hours: 300 Kč, daily 10:00-18:00.

Information: +420 224 233 355, www.mucha.cz.

Getting There: It's at Panská 7, two blocks east of Wenceslas Square.

Length of This Tour: One hour, including time to watch the 30-minute film at the end (usually starts at the top and bottom of the hour).

Starring: The early posters and artistic process of Alphonse Mucha.

THE TOUR BEGINS

▶ *Follow the chronological exhibit, section by section.*

❶ Timeline and Decorative Panels

Entering the museum, look left (in front of the window) to see a timeline of Mucha's life, along with photos showing the artist, his wife, Maruška, and some of the luminaries they hung out with—from painter Paul Gauguin (seated, with no pants, at Mucha's beloved organ) to Czechoslovak president Tomáš Garrigue Masaryk to composer Leoš Janáček.

Mucha's fame was hard-earned. It was the result of innate talent, hard work, and—at a few crucial moments—pure dumb luck. Mucha was born in the Moravian village of Ivančice, and almost from his infancy, he displayed prodigious artistic talent. After studying in Vienna, Mucha rode the train back to his homeland and hopped off where he happened to run out of money: in the Moravian village of Mikulov, where a local aristocrat hired him to decorate a newly built estate. That count's cousin later employed Mucha and was impressed enough to bankroll the young artist's studies in Paris.

Mucha arrived in Paris just in time for the banquet years at the turn of the 20th century. It was a flourishing of world-class artistic and literary talent rarely seen in history—when geniuses like Toulouse-Lautrec, Gauguin, Picasso, Hemingway, Gertrude Stein, and many others were rattling around the grand old city, creating a "bohemian" culture of a very different sort from the one Mucha knew. These artists—whose paths often crossed—found inspiration as they

Alphonse Mucha returned to his homeland from Paris to create the *Slav Epic*.

Alphonse Mucha and the *Slav Epic*

Alphonse Mucha was born in the small Moravian town of Ivančice. He studied in Vienna and Munich, worked for a while in Moravia, then went to Paris to seek his fortune. After suffering as a starving artist, he was hired to design a poster for a play starring the well-known French actress Sarah Bernhardt. Overnight, Mucha was famous. He forged an instantly recognizable style: attractive young women amid flowery designs backed with a halo-like circle. His pastel pretties appeared on magazine covers, wallpaper, carpets, and ad campaigns hawking everything from biscuits to beer. Mucha's florid style helped define what became known as Art Nouveau.

But even as he pursued a lucrative (if superficial) career, Mucha was thinking about his native land. While preparing the Bosnian Pavilion for the Paris Exposition of 1900, he traveled widely through Slavic lands, soaking up the culture, history, and traditions. Inspired to immortalize great moments in Slavic history on a grand scale, Mucha, while on a triumphant tour in America, convinced Chicago industrialist Charles Crane to bankroll his project.

At age 50—after years of living abroad—Mucha returned to his homeland. He rented a château big enough to accommodate both his ego and huge canvases. In 1928, Mucha's lifework—the *Slav Epic*—was unveiled and donated to the city of Prague. A series of 20 thrilling, movie-screen-sized canvases, this visual equivalent of a Wagner opera tells the story of the Slavic people, from their humble beginnings on the Eurasian Steppes to the optimism of the post-WWI era, when Slavic nations created their own modern states (such as Czechoslovakia) for the first time. Mucha paid little attention to actual historical knowledge of his time, choosing instead to draw his own idealized (critics would say outdated, or even distorted) vision of the past. Mucha intended the themes illustrated to be universal, evoking not just Slavic but all human experience.

But the initial response in his homeland was lukewarm. In the experimental age of Dalí and Picasso, Mucha's representational style was out of fashion. Plus, it was highly unusual for an artist of Mucha's stature to go 20 years without the slightest change in personal style. It was as if Mucha froze—or perhaps sacrificed—his evolving artistic genius in order to complete this grandiose vision.

In 1939, German tanks rumbled into Czechoslovakia. The Nazis considered Slavs an inferior race. They arrested the patriot Mucha—then 79 years old—and he was interrogated by the Gestapo. He died a few weeks later. During the war, Mucha's canvases were hidden away and damaged in the process.

In 1963, after years of restoration, the paintings were displayed in the obscure Czech town of Moravský Krumlov, near Mucha's birth-place, where only a handful of visitors came to see them. In 2011, they were properly displayed in Prague's Veletržní Palace. Then, after four years, the paintings went on an immensely popular tour to Japan.

Currently, the *Slav Epic* is back in Moravský Krumlov and will likely be there until 2027. It's scheduled to then move into a specially designed exhibition space in Prague's Savarin Palace, just off Wenceslas Square. (The city of Prague owns the *Slav Epic*, but for decades finding a suitable location has been a challenge.) Check with the ticket desk at the Mucha Museum for the latest updates, and be sure to see this great Czech visual masterpiece if it is on display in town.

experimented with the arts, drugs, and whatever else they could get their hands on.

Across from the photos are several **decorative posters,** which were some of the earliest works that gained Mucha some acclaim. These employ many of the signature flourishes that would define Mucha's style throughout his career: willowy maidens with flowing hair and gowns, curvaceous poses, and flowers in their hair. The ladies intertwine in the foliage around them, framed by Tiffany-glass backdrops and radiating pastel tones. You'll see *The Four Flowers* (framed in Gothic windows), *The Four Times of Day,* and *The Four Arts.* Notice how, rather than the conventional method of depicting each figure with a concrete symbol (such as a paintbrush for painting, or an instrument for music), Mucha simply evokes a mood in each scene. For example, the flowers of the "painting" maiden radiate rainbows.

Philosophically, Mucha believed that art wasn't to be elevated and kept at arm's length in a museum; rather, he wanted it to be shared and experienced in everyday life. These panels were designed to be mass-produced, to decorate urbanites' cramped flats. Mucha enjoyed the idea that, through his works, people could enjoy flowers inside, even in the wintertime. Throughout the collection, you'll see how Mucha's works toe the line between advertising and what we'd more conventionally call "art." As the gap separating "pop culture" and just plain "culture" has blurred even more in our own age, Mucha's works provide an interesting point of reflection.

▶ *The next section is dedicated to...*

❷ Parisian Posters

Turn your attention to the tall, skinny *Gismonda* **poster** at the far end of the room, the result of another extremely lucky stroke for Mucha. It's Paris, on the day after Christmas, 1894. Mucha—the low man on the totem pole at his design firm—is the lone artist on duty, while the more senior designers are enjoying some holiday time off. Unexpectedly, Sarah Bernhardt—perhaps the most famous theater actress who has ever lived—asks for a poster to be designed to promote her new play. In just a week, working under intense pressure, Mucha cranks out this poster, which is plastered all over town on New Year's Day. Mucha becomes, literally, an overnight sensation. When Parisians start stealing the posters for themselves, it's clear Mucha is

Mucha's eye-catching, revolutionary Parisian posters sealed his fame.

on to something. Bernhardt signs him to a six-year contract, and he's the most in-demand artist in town.

The poster was as revolutionary as it was typical of Mucha's emerging style: tall, vertical, hazy pastels, slinky curlicues. Survey the **other posters**—advertising theater presentations (starring Bernhardt and others), art installations, even tobacco (Job).

The posters are lithographs, a printing process popularized in late-19th-century Paris (think Toulouse-Lautrec's ads for cancan shows). The artist draws on a stone slab with a grease crayon (or traces onto a greasy film), then coats the slab with water. The ink sticks to the greasy areas and is repelled by the watery parts. It was easy to crank out cheap (but exquisite) four-color posters—intended as throwaway advertising, but soon accepted as high art.

Think about how, in our age, movie posters (like Drew Struzan's iconic posters for the *Star Wars* and *Indiana Jones* series), album covers, and comic-book characters decorate dorm rooms and rec rooms far more than any other artwork of the past 50 years. Increasingly, mass-produced art—accessible, eye-catching, and linked with fond memories of entertainment—is the art that really matters to the masses.

Before moving on, notice (in the windows) **photos of models** that Mucha posed, lit, photographed, and painstakingly copied for his works. You'll see several figures wearing detailed costumes. As photography was a relatively new medium in Mucha's day, this was a revolutionary tool that would have been unknown to previous generations of artists.

During this same period, Mucha grows more ambitious. He doesn't just do posters—he also designs pavilions for the 1900 Paris World Exposition. A Renaissance man in Art Nouveau times, Mucha dabbles in everything. And he's ready to share his expertise with the world.

▶ *Continuing past the Parisian posters, the room narrows. On the left wall are excerpts from...*

❸ Documents Decoratifs

Mucha is a sensation, and he can't meet the demand all by himself. In keeping with his mission to spread art to the masses, in 1902 Mucha publishes a collection of 72 prints called *Documents Decoratifs,* essentially a how-to manual for Art Nouveau. Notice how, no matter the subject—from furniture to stained glass to jewelry to semi-erotic nudes—Mucha approaches the subject with his consistent (and consistently eye-pleasing) style. This guy literally wrote the book on his chosen art form.

▶ *On the right wall are more posters, but now with Czech themes.*

❹ Czech Posters

Mucha and his wife Maruška meet in Paris and move for a while to the US—mostly to earn money to finance his planned magnum opus, the *Slav Epic*. But in 1910, they return to Bohemia—and get even more caught up in Czech patriotism. These are the waning days of the Austro-Hungarian Empire (which kept the Czech culture and language firmly under its thumb), and the burgeoning Czech National Revival has already inspired generations of Czechs to celebrate what makes their culture unique.

While working on the *Slav Epic* at his Bohemian countryside chateau, Mucha designs posters that commemorate Czech culture while promoting specific events: The Moravian Teachers' Choir took the Czech music of Janáček and others on the road. The Sokol ("Falcon") athletic movement had emerged during Austro-Hungarian times as an important exhibition of Czech strength and pride. And the Lottery of

National Unity (in 1912) was used to raise funds for Czech-language education (in an age when German was the official language and given strongly preferential treatment in schools).

Notice the consistent use of Slavia, a mythical goddess who blesses these proceedings. Mucha's fragile Parisian maidens have become stout Czech peasants and strong workers; when it comes to Slavic women, power equals beauty—strong is sexy.

In comparison, examine the contrasting figures Mucha uses in the lottery poster: The stubborn young girl, eagerly gripping her pencil and pad, dares you to help her learn Czech—and will surely grow into one of the strong women we see elsewhere. But in the hazy background behind her, the goddess Czechia is as withered as the tree she sits upon—wasting away from years of neglect.

At the end of the room—between posters promoting cultural events—is the much-reproduced ***Princess Hyacinth,*** reclining in a chair with a frank, unflinching gaze. This Czech ballet—composed by a Czech, in the Czech language, starring a Czech actress—premiered in the Czech National Theater (a symbol of the Czech National Revival) in 1911...all of which would have been nearly unthinkable in the Austrian town of "Prag" just a few decades earlier.

▶ *Continue into the next room, which you'll circle counterclockwise, starting on your right.*

❺ Paintings

While we've mostly seen Mucha the draftsman so far, he was also a talented painter (the medium he used for his masterpiece, the *Slav Epic*). Find the giant canvas *Star* (also called *Woman in the Wilderness*), in which a starving Russian peasant woman sits and gazes up at a bright

Displays trace Mucha's artistic process.

Detail of *Princess Hyacinth* ballet poster

star. Here Mucha demonstrates his emotional connection to all Slavic peoples. This was painted in 1923, as the Czechs were living one of their historical high-water marks, the post-WWI creation of the state of Czechoslovakia. But at that same time, post-Bolshevik Revolution Russia was suffering from famine—and here, Mucha hasn't forgotten his eastern comrades.

▶ *The area at the end of the hall is a collection of Mucha's...*

❻ Drawings and Pastels

Even his rudimentary sketches demonstrate an innate sense of design—from jewelry to a very early sketch of his stained-glass window of Cyril and Methodius in St. Vitus Cathedral (looking more rigidly geometrical than the final, more fluid version). Look carefully in the showcases in the middle of the room, which display (among other items) pages of books that Mucha illustrated. In the first case, find the Crucifixion that Mucha drew as a precocious eight-year-old. (His mother claimed that he could draw even before he could walk—she gave him a pencil to scrawl artfully on the floor.) In the second case, at the far end, find the banknotes and medals that Mucha designed for the budding nation of Czechoslovakia. Having already earned his fame and fortune, much of Mucha's output in his later years was essentially donating his time and talent to celebrate his homeland and build national pride. In the smaller display cases along the window are Mucha's sketchbooks, offering a glimpse at how he turned small-scale motifs into larger masterworks.

At the end of the room (you've been hearing it this whole time) is an excellent 30-minute **movie** that narrates Mucha's life. It's in English and generally plays at the top and bottom of each hour.

▶ *Finally, circling back the way you came, you'll find items from Mucha's...*

❼ Studio

The desk, easel, and chair (in which Mucha is seated in the most famous portrait photograph of him) came from his studio. On the wall are more photographs of his models, many of them nude.

▶ *After this revealing look at Mucha and his works, consider a visit to the Art Nouveau interiors of the Municipal House, where Mucha designed and painted the Mayor's Salon.*

Prague Castle Tour

Pražský Hrad

For more than a thousand years, Czech leaders—from kings and emperors to Nazis, communists, and presidents—have ruled from Prague Castle. When Christianity arrived in the Czech lands, this promontory overlooking the Vltava River proved a perfect spot for a church and, later, the cathedral. Eventually nobles built their palaces near the castle to compete with the Church for influence on the king. You'll feel like clip-clopping through this neighborhood in a fancy carriage.

Worthwhile sights at this large complex include the castle (grounds, gardens, and Old Royal Palace interior), St. Vitus Cathedral (stained glass and royal tombs), and a castle museum. With more time, you can visit the Basilica of St. George, tour a noble family's private collection (Lobkowicz Palace), wander the Royal Gardens, and more.

Getting There

By Tram: Trams #22 and #23 take you up to the castle (see page 120 for my self-guided tram tour). Catch either tram at Národní Třída (between Wenceslas Square and the National Theater in the New Town), in front of the National Theater (Národní Divadlo, on the riverbank in the New Town), or at Malostranská (the Metro stop in the Lesser Town). After rattling up the hill, trams make three stops near the castle:

Pražský Hrad (Prague Castle) offers the quickest commute to the castle—from the stop, simply walk along U Prašného Mostu and over the bridge to the **northern entrance,** which leads into the castle's Second Courtyard.

Královský Letohrádek (Royal Summer Palace) allows a scenic and relaxed approach through the Royal Gardens to the bridge near the castle's **northern entrance.**

Pohořelec is best if you'd like to start with the Strahov Monastery, then hike 10 minutes down to Castle Square (by way of Loreta Church) and begin your tour there, at the castle's **main entrance.**

By Taxi or Uber: Ask your driver to drop you at either Pražský Hrad or Královský Letohrádek.

By Foot: The fairly steep, three-quarter-mile uphill walk from the river takes about 20 minutes. From the Charles Bridge, follow the

main cobbled road (Mostecká) to the Lesser Town Square, marked by the huge, green-domed Church of St. Nicholas. From there, hike uphill along Nerudova street. After about 10 minutes, a steep lane on the right leads to Castle Square.

Planning Your Time

Minimize the effect of crowds and maximize your enjoyment by following one of these plans.

Early-Bird Visit: Leave your hotel no later than 8:00. Ride the tram (or Uber) to the Pražský Hrad stop, go through the **northern entrance,** and be sure you're in line at the ticket office in the Third Courtyard, across from St. Vitus Cathedral, before 9:00. Once you have your ticket, head to the cathedral as soon as possible after it opens at 9:00, and for a few minutes, you'll have the sacred space to yourself... then, on your way out, you'll pass a noisy human traffic jam of multinational tour groups. Visit the rest of the castle sights at your leisure.

Sneaking in Through a Scenic Route at Peak Times: When it's busy (see "Crowd-Beating Tips" later), a delightful way to get to the castle is to sneak in through a scenic route, allowing you to enjoy an elegant, untouristed dimension of the castle. Ride the tram (or Uber) to the Královský Letohrádek stop and approach the castle via the Royal Gardens. Ideally, arrive at the gardens at 10:00, when the grounds open (closed Nov-March). From there it's a pleasant 20-minute stroll, passing the Renaissance-style Royal Summer Palace and a singing fountain, a ball game hall with decor inspired by Greek mythology, and the now-empty, pseudo-Baroque house of the communist "people's" presidents. As you leave the garden, you'll come to the Powder Bridge, which leads to the castle complex's **northern entrance.**

Afternoon Visit/Adding on Strahov Monastery and Loreta Church: If you're heading to Prague Castle after lunch and want to add on an efficient visit to the sights above the castle, ride the tram to the Pohořelec stop. Tour the Strahov Monastery, then drop by Loreta Church on your way (downhill) to the **Castle Square main entrance** (monastery and church both described in the Sights chapter). By the time you hit Castle Square, the crowds should be thinning out. The only risk is running out of time to enter all the sights by closing time.

Nighttime Visit: The castle is least crowded at night. True, the sights are closed, but the castle grounds are free, safe, peaceful, floodlit, and open late.

ORIENTATION

Cost: Admission to the castle grounds is free, but you need a ticket to enter the sights. The "Basic circuit" ticket (250 Kč) covers the highlights: St. Vitus Cathedral, the Old Royal Palace, the Basilica of St. George, and the Golden Lane. A second "Permanent exhibitions" ticket (200 Kč) adds two sights (the Prague Castle Picture Gallery and *The Story of Prague Castle* exhibit)—read the description on page 101 before buying this add-on. Tickets are good for two days.

Hours: Castle grounds—daily 6:00-22:00; castle sights—daily 9:00-17:00, Nov-March until 16:00; castle gardens—daily 10:00-18:00, closed Nov-March. On Sunday, St. Vitus Cathedral is closed until noon for Mass. The cathedral can close unexpectedly for special services (check www.katedralasvatehovita.cz or call +420 724 933 441).

Information: +420 224 371 111, www.hrad.cz.

Buying Castle Tickets: Inside the castle complex, ticket offices are marked by a green *i*. You'll find one in the Second Courtyard, one in the Third Courtyard (in front of the cathedral), and one at the east end of the complex (near the Golden Lane). Lines can be long at one and nonexistent at the next—they may be shortest at the office in front of the cathedral. Hang on to your ticket; you must present it at each sight. Tickets are not sold online.

Crowd-Beating Tips: Prague Castle is the city's most crowded sight. Peak times are 9:30-14:00 in high season. The most cramped area is the free vestibule inside St. Vitus Cathedral; any sight that you pay to enter—including other parts of the cathedral—will be less jammed.

The shortest lines are typically at the northern entrance (where this tour starts), which you can reach from the Pražský Hrad tram stop or through the scenic Royal Gardens approach; the longest lines are at the main Castle Square entrance.

More Sights at the Castle: Additional sights within the complex are covered by separate tickets and have their own hours: the **St. Vitus Treasury in the Chapel of the Holy Cross** (300 Kč, daily 10:00-18:00, last entry one hour before closing), climbing the **Great South Tower of St. Vitus Cathedral** (150 Kč, daily

10:00-18:00, until 16:00 in winter), and **Lobkowicz Palace** (290 Kč, daily 10:00-18:00, +420 233 312 925, www.lobkowicz.cz).

Tours: An audioguide is available at ticket offices (350 Kč plus 500 Kč deposit). I'd skip it in favor of the tour in this chapter.

Length of This Tour: Seeing the castle complex takes two to three hours; touring Lobkowicz Palace adds another hour. Figure yet another hour to add the Strahov Monastery and Loreta Church (described in the Sights chapter).

Eateries: The castle complex has several forgettable cafés scattered within it, but good eateries are nearby; for listings and a map with locations, see the Eating chapter. I like the scenic, creative café at Lobkowicz Palace.

Starring: Europe's biggest castle, a fine cathedral with a stained-glass Mucha masterpiece, and grand views over the city.

THE TOUR BEGINS

▶ *This tour starts at the bridge just outside the northern entrance, which is easily reached from the Pražský Hrad tram stop or via a longer but pleasant stroll through the Royal Gardens. If approaching from Castle Square, join this tour at stop #2, the Second Courtyard.*

❶ Powder Bridge (Prašný Most)

Before you cross the bridge, survey the scene ahead of you. To your left is the most impressive view of the prickly steeples and flying buttresses of the majestic St. Vitus Cathedral, which stands in the middle of the medieval iceberg called Prague Castle. It's a 1,900-foot-long series of courtyards, churches, and palaces, covering 750,000 square feet—by some measures, the largest castle on earth. Crossing the bridge (actually a landfill), look down into the abysmal Stag Moat (Jelení příkop) that naturally protects the fortress from the north.

The stoic **guards** at this northern entrance make a great photo-op, as does the changing of the guard (on the hour). In fact, there's a guard-changing ceremony at every gate: top, bottom, and north. The biggest, but also most crowded, ceremony and music occurs at noon, at the top gate by Castle Square.

Prague Castle Tour

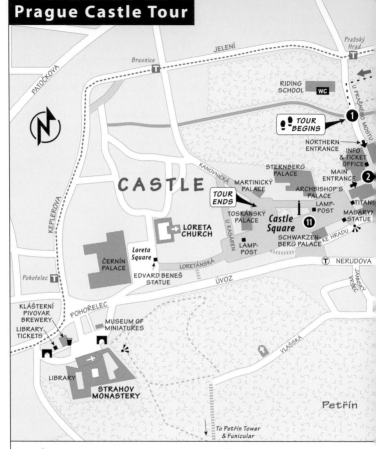

1. Powder Bridge
2. Second Courtyard
3. St. Vitus Cathedral
4. Third Courtyard
5. Old Royal Palace
6. Story of Prague Castle Exhibit
7. Basilica of St. George
8. Golden Lane
9. Lobkowicz Palace
10. Ramparts Garden
11. Castle Square

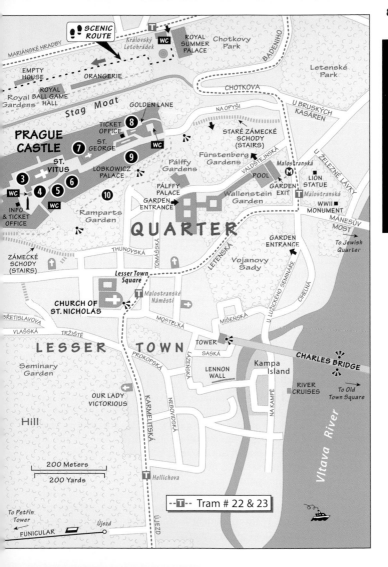

SCENIC ROUTE

MARIÁNSKÉ HRADBY

Královský Letohrádek

WC

ROYAL SUMMER PALACE

Chotkovy Park

BADENIHO

Letenské Park

EMPTY HOUSE

ORANGERIE

CHOTKOVA

U BRUSKÝCH KASÁREN

ROYAL BALL GAME Gardens HALL

Stag Moat

GOLDEN LANE

NA OPYŠI

PRAGUE CASTLE

TICKET OFFICE

8

STARÉ ZÁMECKÉ SCHODY (STAIRS)

U ŽELEZNÉ LÁVKY

7

ST. GEORGE

9

Fürstenberg Gardens

Pálffy Gardens

VALDŠTEJNSKÁ

Malostranská

M

POOL

LION STATUE

ST. VITUS

3

LOBKOWICZ PALACE

GARDEN EXIT

Malostranská

4

5

6

PÁLFFY PALACE

Wallenstein Garden

WC

10

GARDEN ENTRANCE

WC

INFO & TICKET OFFICE

Ramparts Garden

WWII MONUMENT

MÁNESŮV MOST

QUARTER

To Jewish Quarter

ZÁMECKÉ SCHODY (STAIRS)

THUNOVSKÁ

GARDEN ENTRANCE

TOMÁŠSKÁ

LETENSKÁ

Vojanovy Sady

Lesser Town Square

Malostranské Náměstí

CHIMELNÁ

BŘETISLAVOVA

CHURCH OF ST. NICHOLAS

VLAŠSKÁ

TRŽIŠTĚ

MOSTECKÁ

MÍŠEŇSKÁ

LESSER TOWN

PROKOPSKÁ

UZENSKÁ

SASKÁ

TOWER

CHARLES BRIDGE

Seminary Garden

LENNON WALL

Kampa Island

OUR LADY VICTORIOUS

KARMELITSKÁ

NEBOVIDSKÁ

RIVER CRUISES

To Old Town Square

Hill

NA KAMPĚ

U LUŽICKÉHO SEMINÁŘE

Vltava River

200 Meters

200 Yards

T Hellichova

ÚJEZD

--T-- Tram # 22 & 23

To Petřín Tower

FUNICULAR

Újezd

Photo-op with palace guard

Changing of the guard happens on the hour.

▶ *Walk through the double gate and emerge into the Second Courtyard. To your right is an information center where you can buy your ticket (or, if lines are long, try the one in the Third Courtyard, then come back to start the tour).*

❷ Second Courtyard

During the 18th century, Empress Maria Theresa commissioned her favorite Italian architect to connect the disparate buildings in the castle grounds into a unified Neoclassical whole. Notice how the uniform facade lacks the expressiveness of Baroque seen elsewhere in town. On the eve of the French Revolution, fancy facades were suddenly considered ostentatious, as aristocrats no longer wanted to display wealth and status on the outside. But even in this sea of rectangular uniformity there is an element that fits with Prague: the curved upper line over the windows that harks back to the flowing Baroque dynamism of the preceding era.

Although Maria Theresa never resided here, the imposing—and to this day largely empty—complex was meant to project the aura of undisputed Habsburg power. This included painting the whole thing in the Habsburgs' favorite shade of yellow. Locals still feel uncomfortable in these "Viennese" surroundings and rush through the courtyard to take cover in one of the blessedly medieval interiors.

Before you do the same, note the fountain and Renaissance well in the middle of the square.

Just to the left of the well, the modern green awning (with the golden-winged griffin) marks the entrance to the **offices of the Czech president.** If the president is in town, his flag flies over the roof at the opposite end of the square.

▶ *Now walk through the passageway (to the left of the president's office) that leads into the Third Courtyard. There you'll see the impressive facade of St. Vitus Cathedral. Even without a ticket, tourists can step into the church entryway for a crowded view of the nave (and a bit of the Mucha stained glass)—but it's worth paying to see the whole church.*

❸ St. Vitus Cathedral (Katedrála Sv. Víta)

This Roman Catholic cathedral is the Czech national church—it's where kings were crowned, royalty have their tombs, the relics of saints are venerated, and the crown jewels are kept. Since AD 920, a church has stood on this spot, marking the very origins of the Czech nation.

❶ **Entrance Facade:** The two soaring towers of this Gothic wonder rise 270 feet. The ornate facade features pointed arches, elaborate tracery, Flamboyant pinnacles, a rose window, a dozen statues of saints, and gargoyles sticking out their tongues.

So what's up with the four guys in modern suits carved into the stone, as if supporting the big, round window on their shoulders? They're the architects and builders who finished the church six centuries after it was started. Even though church construction got underway in 1344, wars, plagues, and the reforms of Jan Hus conspired to stall its completion. Finally, fueled by a burst of Czech nationalism, Prague's top church was finished in 1929 for the 1,000th Jubilee anniversary of St. Wenceslas. The entrance facade and towers were the last parts to be finished.

▶ *Enter the cathedral. If it's not too crowded in the free entrance area, work your way to the middle of the church for a good...*

❷ **View Down the Nave:** The church is huge—more than 400 feet long and 100 feet high—and flooded with light. Notice the intricate "net" vaulting on the ceiling, especially at the far end. It's the signature feature of the church's chief architect, Peter Parler (who also built the Charles Bridge).

▶ *Now make your way through the crowds and pass through the ticket turnstile (left of the roped-off area). The third window on the left wall is worth a close look.*

St. Vitus Cathedral

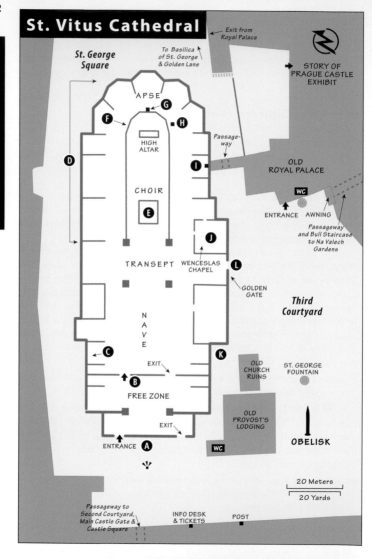

Exit from Royal Palace

STORY OF PRAGUE CASTLE EXHIBIT

St. George Square

To Basilica of St. George & Golden Lane

APSE

G

F

H

HIGH ALTAR

D

Passageway

OLD ROYAL PALACE

I

WC

ENTRANCE   AWNING

CHOIR

E

Passageway and Bull Staircase to Na Valech Gardens

J

TRANSEPT

WENCESLAS CHAPEL

L

GOLDEN GATE

Third Courtyard

N A V E

C

EXIT

B

FREE ZONE

K

OLD CHURCH RUINS

ST. GEORGE FOUNTAIN

OLD PROVOST'S LODGING

EXIT

ENTRANCE **A**

WC

OBELISK

20 Meters

20 Yards

Passageway to Second Courtyard, Main Castle Gate & Castle Square

INFO DESK & TICKETS

POST

A Entrance Facade

B View down the Nave

C Mucha Stained-Glass Window

D Old Church

E Royal Mausoleum

F Relief of Prague

G Tomb of St. Vitus

H Tomb of St. John of Nepomuk

I Royal Oratory

J Wenceslas Chapel

K Tower Entrance

L Last Judgment Mosaic

C Mucha Stained-Glass Window: This masterful 1931 Art Nouveau window was designed by Czech artist Alphonse Mucha and executed by a stained-glass craftsman (if you like this, you'll love the Mucha Museum in the New Town).

Mucha's window was created to celebrate the birth of the Czech nation and the life of Wenceslas. The main scene (in the four central panels) shows Wenceslas as an impressionable child kneeling at the feet of his Christian grandmother, St. Ludmila. She spreads her arms and teaches him to pray. Wenceslas would grow up to champion Christianity, uniting the Czech people.

Above Wenceslas are the two saints who first brought Christianity to the region: Cyril (the monk in a black hood holding the Bible) and

Alphonse Mucha celebrated the birth of his nation and the life of Wenceslas with this window.

St. Vitus Cathedral is where Czech kings have been crowned and buried.

his older brother, Methodius (with a beard and bishop's garb). They baptize a kneeling convert.

Follow their story in the side panels, starting in the upper left. Around AD 860 (back when Ludmila was just a girl), these two Greek missionary brothers arrive in Moravia to preach. The pagan Czechs have no written language to read the Bible, so (in the next scene below), Cyril bends at his desk to design the necessary alphabet (Glagolitic, which later developed into Cyrillic), while Methodius meditates. In the next three scenes, they travel to Rome and present their newly translated Bible to the pope. But Cyril falls ill, and Methodius watches his kid brother die.

Methodius carries on (in the upper right), becoming bishop of the Czech lands. Next, he's arrested for heresy for violating the pure Latin Bible. He's sent to a lonely prison. When he's finally set free, he retires to a monastery, where he dies mourned by the faithful.

But that's just the beginning of the story. At the bottom center are two beautiful (classic Mucha) maidens, representing the bright future of the Czech and Slovak peoples. (And on the bottom, the tasteful little ad for *Banka Slavie,* which paid for the work, is hardly noticeable.)

▸ *Continue circulating around the church, following the one-way, clockwise route.*

❿ Old Church: Just after the transept, notice there's a slight incline in the floor. That's because the church was constructed in two distinct stages. You're entering the older, 14th-century Gothic section. The front half (where you came in) is a Neo-Gothic extension that was finally completed in the 1920s (which is why much of the stained glass has a modern design). For 400 years—as the nave was being extended—a temporary wall kept the functional altar area protected from the construction zone.

▸ *In the choir area (on your right), soon after the transept, look for the big, white marble tomb surrounded by a black iron fence.*

⓫ Royal Mausoleum: This contains the remains of the first Habsburgs to rule Bohemia, including Ferdinand I, his wife, Anne, and Maximilian II. The tomb dates from 1590, when Prague was a major Habsburg city.

▸ *Just after the choir, as you begin to circle around the back of the altar, watch on your right for the fascinating, carved-wood...*

Part of the church has modern stained glass.

Royal Mausoleum—a tomb for kings

❻ Relief of Prague: This depicts the aftermath of the Battle of White Mountain, when the Protestant King Frederic escaped over the Charles Bridge (before it had any statues). Carved in 1630, the relief gives you a peek at old Prague. Find the Týn Church (far left) and St. Vitus Cathedral (far right), which was half-built at that time. The old city walls—now replaced by the main streets of the city—stand strong. The Jewish Quarter is the flood-prone zone along the riverside below the bridge on the left—land no one else wanted. The weir system on the river—the wooden barriers that help control its flow—survives to this day.

▶ *Circling around the high altar, you'll see various...*

Tombs in the Apse: Among the graves of medieval kings and bishops is that of **❼ St. Vitus,** shown as a young man clutching a book and gazing up to heaven. Why is this huge cathedral dedicated to this rather obscure saint, who was martyred in Italy in AD 303 and never set foot in Bohemia? A piece of Vitus' arm bone (a holy relic) was supposedly acquired by Wenceslas I in 925. Wenceslas built a church to house the relic on this spot, attracting crowds of pilgrims. Vitus became quite popular throughout the Germanic and Slavic lands, and revelers danced on his feast day. (He's now the patron saint of dancers.)

A few steps farther, the big silvery tomb with the angel-borne canopy honors **❽ St. John of Nepomuk.** Locals claim it has more than a ton of silver.

Just past the tomb, on the wall of the choir (on the right), is another finely carved, circa-1630 **wood relief** depicting an event that took place right here in St. Vitus: Protestant nobles trash the cathedral's Catholic icons after their (short-lived) victory.

Ahead on the left, look up at the **❾ royal oratory,** a box supported

17th-century relief shows a "bridge" of weirs.

St. John of Nepomuk with halo of stars

by busy late-Gothic, vine-like ribs. This private box, connected to the king's apartment by an outside corridor, let the king attend Mass in his jammies. The underside of the balcony is morbidly decorated with dead vines and tree branches, suggesting the pessimism common in the late Gothic period, when religious wars and Ottoman invasions threatened the Czech lands.

▶ *From here, walk 25 paces and look left through the crowds and door to see the richly decorated chapel containing the tomb of St. Wenceslas. Two roped-off doorways give visitors a look inside. The best view is from the second one, around the corner and to the left, in the transept.*

❶ **Wenceslas Chapel:** This fancy chapel is the historic heart of the church. It contains the tomb of St. Wenceslas, patron saint of the Czech nation; it's where Bohemia's kings were crowned, and it houses (but rarely displays) the Bohemian crown jewels. The chapel walls are paneled with big slabs of precious and semiprecious stones. The jewel-toned stained-glass windows (from the 1950s) admit a soft light. The chandelier is exceptional. The place feels medieval.

The tomb of St. Wenceslas is a colored-stone coffin topped with an ark. Above the chapel's altar is a statue of Wenceslas, bearing a lance and a double-eagle shield. He's flanked by (painted) angels and the four patron saints of the Czech people. Above Wenceslas are portraits of Charles IV (who built the current church) and his beautiful wife. On the wall to the left of the altar, frescoes depict the saint's life, including the episode where angels arrive with crosses to arm the holy warrior.

For centuries, Czech kings were crowned right here in front of Wenceslas' red-draped coffin. The new king was handed a royal scepter, orb, and sword, and fitted with the jeweled St. Wenceslas crown

The Wenceslas Chapel, with Wenceslas' tomb (right), is where Czech kings were crowned.

made for Charles IV. These precious objects are kept locked away behind a door in the corner of the chapel. The door (and the iron safe behind it) has seven locks whose seven keys are held by seven bigwigs (including the Czech president), who must all meet here when someone needs to get inside.

▶ Leave the cathedral, turn left (past the WC), and survey the...

❹ Third Courtyard

The **obelisk** was erected in 1928—a single piece of granite celebrating the 10th anniversary of the establishment of Czechoslovakia and commemorating the soldiers who fought for its independence. It was originally much taller but broke in transit—an inauspicious start for a nation destined to last only 70 years.

From here, you get a great look at the sheer size of St. Vitus Cathedral and its fat green **tower** (325 feet tall). Up there is the Czech Republic's biggest **bell** (16.5 tons, from 1549), nicknamed "Zikmund." In June 2002 it cracked, and two months later the worst flood in recorded history hit the city—the locals saw this as a sign. You can view the bell as you climb up the 287 steps of the tower to the observation deck at the top (**🅚 tower tickets and entry** near sculpture of St. George—a 1960s replica of the 13th-century original).

It's easy to find the church's **Golden Gate** (for centuries the cathedral's main entry)—look for the glittering **🅛 14th-century mosaic of the Last Judgment.** The modern, cosmopolitan, and ahead-of-his-time Charles IV commissioned this monumental decoration in 1370 in the Italian style. Jesus oversees the action, as some go to heaven and some go to hell. The Czech king and queen kneel directly beneath Jesus and six patron saints. On coronation day, royalty would walk under this arch, a reminder to them (and their subjects) that even those holding great power are not above God's judgment.

Across from the Golden Gate, in the corner, notice the copper, scroll-like **awning** supported by bulls. This leads to a lovely garden just below the castle.

▶ *In the corner of the Third Courtyard, near the copper awning, is the entrance to the Old Royal Palace. In the lobby, there's a WC with a window shared by the men's and women's sections—meet your partner to enjoy the view.*

🅔 Old Royal Palace (Starý Královský Palác)

Since the ninth century, this has been the seat of the Bohemian princes. The highlight of the palace building (dating from the 12th century) is the large **Vladislav Hall**—200 feet long, with an impressive vaulted ceiling of vine-shaped (late-Gothic) tracery. This hall, used by the old nobility, served many purposes. It could be filled with market stalls, letting aristocrats shop without going into town. It was big enough for jousts—even the staircase (which you'll use as you exit) was designed to let a mounted soldier gallop in. Beginning in the 1500s, nobles met here to elect the king. The tradition survived into modern times. As recently as the 1990s, the Czech parliament crowded into this room to elect their president.

On your immediate right, enter the two small Renaissance rooms known as the **"Czech Office."** From these rooms (empty today except for their 17th-century porcelain heaters), two governors used to oversee the Czech lands for the Habsburgs in Vienna. Head for the far room, wrapped in windows. In 1618, angry Czech Protestant nobles poured into these rooms and threw the two Catholic governors out the window. An old law actually permits this act—called

The Old Royal Palace, with Vladislav Hall, is one of several sights you can pay to visit.

defenestration—which usually targets bad politicians. An old print on the glass panel shows the third of Prague's many defenestrations. The two governors suffered only one broken arm and bruised egos, yet this event kicked off the huge and lengthy Thirty Years' War.

As you reenter the main hall, go to the far end and out on the **balcony** for a sweeping view of Prague. Then head for the door immediately opposite. It opens into the **Diet Hall,** with a fine Gothic ceiling, a crimson throne, and benches for the nobility who once served as the high court. Notice the balcony on the left where scribes recorded the proceedings (without needing to mix with the aristocrats). The portraits on the walls depict Habsburg rulers, including Maria Theresa, and Joseph II dressed up as George Washington (both wore fashionable 18th-century attire). The display case on the right contains replicas of the Czech crown jewels.

Return to the main hall; the next door to your right is the exit. Head down those horseback stairs. As you exit outside, pause at the door you just came through to consider the subtle yet racy little Renaissance knocker. Go ahead—play with it for a little sex in the palace (be gentle).

▶ *The next sight requires the extra "Permanent exhibitions" ticket; if you don't have one, skip down to the Basilica of St. George.*

Otherwise, as you exit the Royal Palace, hook left around the side of the building and backtrack a few steps uphill to find stairs leading down to...

❻ *The Story of Prague Castle* Exhibit (Příběh Pražského Hradu)

This museum of old artifacts (with good English descriptions) is your best look at castle history and its kings, all housed in the cool Gothic cellars of the Old Royal Palace. Throughout the exhibit, models of the castle show how it grew over the centuries.

Origins (Room 1): In this low-ceilinged medieval room, you'll learn about prehistoric finds (mammoth bones) and the first settlers (c. 800), churches, and fortifications, and see ivory hunting horns of the first kings.

Patron Saints (Room 2): Czechs trace their origins as a people to several early saints. The first was St. Wenceslas, and you can admire (what may be) his actual chain-mail tunic and helmet. He was raised Christian by his grandmother, Ludmila (view her supposed clothes), and went on to found the original St. Vitus church. St. John of Nepomuk (no artifacts here) lies buried in the church's most ornate tomb.

Archaeological Finds (Room 3): Look through the metal floor to see the foundations of the 12th-century palace. An adjoining room displays ecclesiastical gear, church documents, and (upstairs) bones from early funerals.

Golden Age of Bohemia (Room 4): This large hall hosts numerous artifacts from 1200 through 1400. First come the kings of the Přemysl family (including Ottokar II), then the dynasty of Charles IV and his IV wives.

Habsburg Rulers (Room 5): With Bohemia under Austrian rule, Prague eventually declined. But Emperor Rudolf II moved the Habsburg court for one last time from Vienna to Prague (1583-1612), bringing with him current art styles (Mannerism—the transition from Renaissance to Baroque) and leading-edge scientists (astronomers Tycho Brahe and Johannes Kepler).

A display on the Czech coronation ceremony (always held in St. Vitus) includes fine replicas of the Bohemian crown jewels (the originals are exhibited only on special occasions). They're a reminder that Prague Castle has been the center of the Czech state for more than a millennium.

▶ *Directly across the courtyard from the rear buttresses of St. Vitus is a very old church with a pretty red facade. This is the...*

❼ Basilica of St. George (Bazilika Sv. Jiří)

Step into one of the oldest structures at Prague Castle to see this re-created Romanesque church (a product of a 19th-century "purification" that removed the layers of Baroque) and the burial place of Czech royalty. The church was founded by Wenceslas' dad before 920, and the present structure dates from the 12th century. (Its Baroque facade and side chapel that survived the purification came later.) Inside, the place is beautiful in its simplicity. Notice the characteristic thick walls and rounded arches. In those early years, building techniques were not yet advanced enough to use those arches for the ceiling—it's made of wood instead.

This was the royal burial place before St. Vitus was built, so the tombs here contain the remains of the earliest Czech kings. Climb the stairs that frame either side of the altar to study the area around the apse. St. Wenceslas' grandmother, Ludmila, was reburied here in 925. Her stone tomb is just to the right of the altar. Inside the archway leading to her tomb, look for her portrait. Holding a branch and a book, she looks quite cultured for a 10th-century woman.

As you exit the church, you'll pass some small exhibits about the layers of history at this site.

The red-hued Basilica of St. George

The basilica's 12th-century interior

▶ *Continue walking downhill. Notice the basilica's gorgeous Renais-sance side entrance, with St. George fighting the dragon in the tym-panum. Next you'll see the basilica's Romanesque nave and towers—a strong contrast to the lavish painted Baroque facade. To your right, tucked together, you'll see the palaces of Catholic nobility who wanted to be both close to power and able to band together should the Protes-tants grab the upper hand. Take a left once you have passed the apse of the St. George Basilica, then turn right and then left again to stroll through the...*

❽ Golden Lane

This medieval merchant street was once lined with the former resi-dences of soldiers and craftsmen. Today it's filled with touristy shops.

▶ *At the end of the Golden Lane, walk down the stairway in a tunnel and, keeping the former prison tower to your left, make a sharp right turn through a small gate. Walk across a courtyard and exit to the left to face the...*

❾ Lobkowicz Palace (Lobkowiczký Palác)

This palace, rated ▲▲ and covered by a separate ticket, displays the private collection of a prominent Czech noble family, including paintings, ceramics, and musical scores. The Lobkowiczes' property was confiscated twice in the 20th century: first by the Nazis at the beginning of World War II, and then by the communists in 1948. In 1990, William Lobkowicz, then a Boston real estate broker, returned to Czechoslovakia to fight a legal battle to reclaim his family's prop-erty and, eventually, to restore the castles and palaces to their former state. The care that went into creating this museum, the collection's variety, and the personal insight it offers into Czech nobility make the Lobkowicz worth an hour of your time.

Members of the Lobkowicz family (including William) narrate the delightful, included audioguide. If you visit, use the map that comes with your ticket to focus on the highlights:

Second-Floor Landing and Room B: As you pass by the por-traits of Lobkowicz's ancestors, listen to their stories, including that of Polyxena, whose determination saved the two Catholic governors de-fenestrated next door (according to family legend, she hid the bruised officials under the folds of her skirt).

The "Old Castle Stairs" afford a scenic journey down from the castle.

Room G: The family loved music. See their instruments, including old lutes. There's the manuscript of Beethoven's *Eroica* symphony (with his last-minute changes). The piece was dedicated to his sponsor—Prince Lobkowicz (see his portrait)—and premiered at the Lobkowicz Palace in Vienna. Nearby is Mozart's handwritten re-orchestration of Handel's *Messiah*.

Rooms H-J: The highlights of the museum's paintings include Pieter Bruegel the Elder's magnificently preserved *Haymaking* (1565). It's one of the earliest entirely secular landscape paintings in Europe, showing an idyllic and almost heroic connection between peasants and nature.

▶ *Once you're done touring the palace, you can exit the castle complex through the gate at the bottom (eastern) end of the castle. A scenic rampart just below the lower gate offers a commanding view of the city. From there you can either head to the Malostranská tram/Metro station and riverbank or loop around to Castle Square (where this tour continues).*

To reach Malostranská station, *follow the crowds down the 700-some steps of a steep lane called Staré Zámecké Schody ("Old Castle*

*Stairs"). **To continue this tour** (or to reach Strahov Monastery), take a hard right as you leave the castle gate, and stroll through the long, delightful...*

⑩ Ramparts Garden (Zahrada Na Valech)

This garden comes with commanding views of the city below (free, daily 10:00-18:00 or later, closed Nov-March). Along the way, notice the Modernist layout of the garden, designed by Jože Plečnik of Slovenia. Halfway through the long park is a circular viewpoint. At roughly the same distance under the brick wall of the Royal Palace, find a Baroque column commemorating the miraculous survival of the defenestrated overlords. As you exit the garden at the far end through a narrow gate on top of a wide, monumental staircase, notice the cool wolf-snout design of the adjacent doorknob, another Plečnik trademark.

▶ *Make your way into...*

⑪ Castle Square (Hradčanské Náměstí)

Castle Square was the focal point of premodern power. The **Fighting Titans** sculpture, depicting two triumphant gladiators, marks the main entry into the residence of Czech kings. The archbishop lived (and still lives) in the **Archbishop's Palace**—the ornate, white-and-yellow Rococo building with the oversized facade. Above the doorway is the family coat of arms of the archbishop that built this palace: three white goose necks in a red field.

Closer to you, near the overlook, the statue of a man in a business suit (marked *TGM*) honors the father of modern Czechoslovakia: **Tomáš Garrigue Masaryk.** At the end of World War I, Masaryk—a university professor—united the Czechs and Slovaks into one nation and became its first president.

Entertaining bands play regularly by the Masaryk statue in the mornings and early afternoons. (If the Prague Castle Orchestra is playing, say hello to friendly, mustachioed Josef, and consider buying the group's CD—it's terrific.)

On the left side of the square, behind the statue, the building with a step-gable roofline is **Schwarzenberg Palace,** today an art museum with a collection of Renaissance, Baroque, and Rococo paintings and sculpture. Notice the envelope-shaped patterns stamped on the

Musicians perform regularly on Castle Square.   The plague column—a token of gratitude

exterior. These Renaissance-era adornments etched into wet stucco—called sgraffito—decorate buildings throughout the castle and all over Prague.

The dark gray Baroque sculpture in the middle of the square is a **plague column.** Erected as a token of gratitude to Mary and the saints for saving the population from epidemic disease, these columns are an integral part of the main squares of many Habsburg towns.

Two more palaces are worth looking at. At the far-right corner of the square, past the plague column, is the delightful **Martinický Palace,** with delicate Renaissance portals and detailed figural sgraffito depicting the feats of biblical Joseph and mythic Hercules. The pastel **Toskánský Palace** at the western end of the square is a beautifully balanced example of Baroque palatial architecture.

▶ *From the top corner of Toskánský Palace, you can either continue up along Loretánská street to the Loreta Church and Strahov Monastery (both described in the Sights chapter) or take the scenic staircase on the left down to the top of Nerudova street in the Lesser Town. The Pohořelec tram stop is across from Strahov Monastery.*

Sights

These sights are arranged by neighborhood for handy sightseeing. Remember that Prague started out as four towns—the Old Town and New Town on the east side of the river, and the Castle Quarter and Lesser Town on the west—and it's still helpful for sightseers to think of the city that way. I've also included a worthwhile sight outside of the city center.

When you see a 📖 in a listing, it means the sight is described in greater detail in one of my self-guided walks or tours. A 🎧 means a sight is also covered on my free Prague City Walk audio tour (via my Rick Steves Audio Europe app—see page 11).

Prague Sights

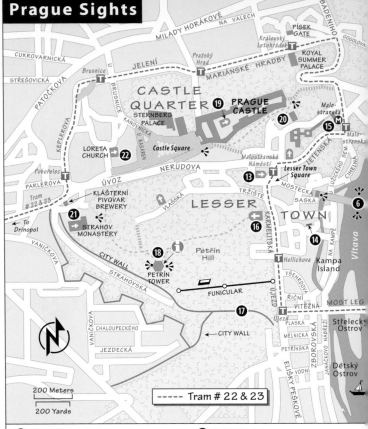

1 Old Town Hall Tower

2 Týn Church

3 Church of St. James

4 Havelská Market

5 Klementinum

6 Charles Bridge

7 Museum of Medieval Art

8 Cold War Museum

9 Mucha Museum

10 Museum of Communism

11 Municipal House & Powder Tower

12 To Dancing House, National Memorial-Heydrich Terror & Vyšehrad Fortress

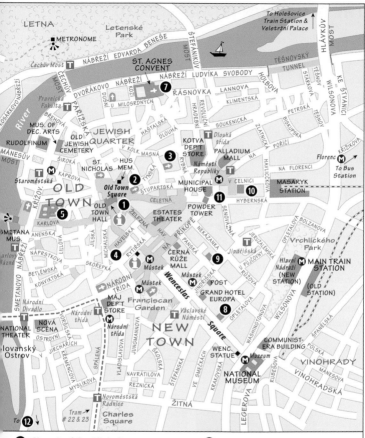

- ⑬ Church of St. Nicholas
- ⑭ Lennon Wall
- ⑮ Wallenstein Palace Garden
- ⑯ Church of Our Lady Victorious
- ⑰ Monument to Victims of Communism & Hunger Wall
- ⑱ Petřín Tower
- ⑲ St. Vitus Cathedral
- ⑳ Lobkowicz Palace
- ㉑ Strahov Monastery & Library
- ㉒ Loreta Church

THE OLD TOWN (STARÉ MĚSTO)

All the sights described here are within a 10-minute walk of the magnificent Old Town Square.

🎧 My Prague City Walk audio tour covers some of these sights; see page 11 for details.

▲▲▲Old Town Square (Staroměstské Náměstí)

Prague's Old Town Square—a perfectly preserved living postcard—is the focal point of most tourist visits. The central statues, honoring Jan Hus and the Virgin Mary, are surrounded by an architectural parade of picturesque buildings, including the Old Town Hall.

📖 See the Old Town & Charles Bridge Walk chapter.

Old Town Hall Tower and Tour

While this building's most popular feature is its Astronomical Clock, you can pay to see other sights inside. Enter to the left of the Astronomical Clock, where you'll find a TI, pay WC, and a bank of elevators. One ticket (sold on floors 1 and 3) covers the tour of the Old Town Hall (you'll see a few sterile rooms and the workings of the Astronomical Clock), as well as the trip up the tower by elevator (from floor 3) for the big view.

▶ *300 Kč for Old Town Hall and tower ascent, discount for advance purchase online; open Tue-Sun 9:00-21:00, Mon from 11:00, shorter hours Jan-March; 45-minute Town Hall tours usually 4/day in English at 10:00, 12:00, 14:00, and 16:00—preregister at ticket office; +420 775 400 052, www.prague.eu.*

Ride Old Town Hall's elevator for a view.

Týn Church's interior—Hussite and Catholic

▲Týn Church

The twin, multiturreted, fairy-tale Gothic towers of the Church of Our Lady Before Týn (its full name) loom over the Old Town Square. While every tourist snaps a photo of this church, consider stepping inside, too. Due to its complex history—first Catholic, then the main Hussite (Protestant) church, then Catholic again—it has an elaborately decorated interior.

　📖 See page 23 of the Old Town & Charles Bridge Walk chapter.

▲Church of St. James (Kostel Sv. Jakuba)

This fine old medieval church, redecorated head-to-toe in exuberant Baroque, features gilded woodwork, bombastic frescoes, and the Madonna Pietatis relic.

　📖 See page 25 of the Old Town & Charles Bridge Walk chapter.

▲Havelská Market

This open-air marketplace is dominated by produce on weekdays; on weekends you'll find more souvenirs, puppets, and toys.

　📖 See page 33 of the Old Town & Charles Bridge Walk chapter.

▲Klementinum

The Czech Republic's massive National Library borders touristy Karlova street. The contrast could not be more stark: Step out of the most souvenir-packed stretch of Central Europe, and enter the meditative silence of high medieval culture.

Jesuits built the Klementinum in the 1600s to house a new college. The building became a library in the early 1700s, forming the historic nucleus of the National and University Library, which is now six million volumes strong.

While much of the Klementinum building is simply a vast modern library, its magnificent original Baroque Library and Observatory Tower are open to the public by tour (45 minutes, in English). You'll see the ornate library with its many centuries-old books, fancy ceilings with Jesuit leaders and saints overseeing the pursuit of knowledge, and Josef II—the enlightened Habsburg emperor—looking on from the far end. Then you'll climb 172 steps up the Observatory Tower, learning how early astronomers charted the skies over Prague. The tour finishes with a grand Prague view from the top.

The Klementinum, built in the 17th century, has a fine Baroque library.

▶ *300 Kč; English-language tours depart daily every half-hour 10:00-17:30, shorter hours off-season; +420 733 129 252, www.prague.eu/klementinum. Strolling down Karlova, turn at the intersection with Liliová through an archway into the Klementinum's courtyard.*

▲▲▲Charles Bridge (Karlův Most)

Prague's landmark icon—connecting the two halves of the city across the Vltava River and lined with statues of Czech saints—is one of Europe's most famous bridges and one of its best public spaces. Day and night, the bridge bustles with buskers, tourists, street vendors, school groups, impromptu concerts...and, occasionally, a few Czechs.

📖 See page 36 of the Old Town & Charles Bridge Walk chapter.

Bridge Towers Climb: You can climb the towers on either end of the Charles Bridge. The tower on the Old Town side (Staroměstská Mostecká Věž, 138 steps) rewards you with great city views, with the best lighting early in the day. On the Lesser Town side (Malostranská Mostecká Věž, 146 steps), you get good views of the bridge, the neighborhood rooftops, and the castle, with the best lighting late in the day.

▶ *150 Kč to climb each tower, daily 9:00-21:00, April-May and Sept 10:00-19:00, Oct-March until 18:00.*

The iconic Charles Bridge, lined with statues, is atmospheric by night or day.

▲▲▲ Jewish Quarter (Josefov)

The Jewish Quarter is the best place in Europe to learn about this important culture and faith interwoven in the fabric of Central and Eastern Europe. Within a three-block radius, several original synagogues, a cemetery, and other landmarks survive, today collected into one big, well-presented sight that can be seen with a single ticket.

📖 See the Jewish Quarter Tour chapter.

▲▲ Museum of Medieval Art
(Středověké umění v Čechách a Střední Evropě)

Prague flourished in the 14th century, and the city has amassed an impressive collection of altarpieces and paintings from that age. Today this art is housed in the tranquil former Convent of St. Agnes, which was founded in the 13th century by a Czech princess-turned-nun as the first hospital in Prague. A visit here is your best chance to see exquisite medieval art in Prague. Here are some highlights:

Aspects of Mary (Room A): The room features many variations on the mother of Jesus, who was adored in medieval Europe. You'll see statues and paintings of her smiling, sitting, or standing; being thoughtful, playful, or majestic; with or without a crown; and nearly always cradling her baby. The first works date from the early 1200s, when this place was a world of women—the Convent of St. Agnes.

Vyšší Brod Paintings (Room B): These gold-backed paintings (from around 1350) tell the story of Christ, medieval-style. In the *Annunciation,* the angel kneels before Mary and announces (you can actually read his words) *Ave gratia plena…*"Hail, full of grace." In the *Nativity,* Mary gives birth in a flimsy, and crudely drawn, shack. But the artist, known only as the Master of Vyšší Brod (the monastery where these panels originated), is experimenting with Italian-style perspective—there's a definite foreground (the couple with water basin) and background (grazing animals).

Master Theodoric (Room C): A half-dozen paintings here give a snapshot of Prague's golden age. Around 1350, Emperor Charles IV hired Theodoric of Prague—the country's first "name" artist—to paint 129 saints, of which a few have been moved here. These saints are massive. They're life-size (or bigger) and zoomed in to show them from the waist up, as if they're peering out of windows.

In the second painting, Charlemagne—the first Holy Roman Emperor—holds the same coronation objects used by Charles IV: golden scepter, orb, and shield with the double-headed eagle. The hand of Theodoric is everywhere: his signature beard style, thick outlines, brilliant colors, and "soft-focus" features.

The Beautiful Style (Rooms G, H): These Madonna statues are deliberately graceful, with delicate, curved lines. Mary smiles sweetly, her body sways seductively, her deeply creased robe is luxuriant, and Jesus squirms playfully in her arms. Worshippers were treated to these happy, once colorfully painted, and "beautiful" images of an

Museum of Medieval Art has many Marys…

…and Charlemagne, forerunner of Czech kings.

Exploring the St. Agnes Convent

In 1233, Prague's Princess Agnes, the daughter of the Czech king, met a famous Italian nun—Clare, a friend of the charismatic St. Francis of Assisi. Agnes established a branch of the Poor Clare nuns here in Prague. She built this complex (located on the right bank of the river, near the Jewish Quarter), consisting of a convent, churches, and the city's first hospital—all of it state-of-the-art.

Courtyard: Circle the courtyard counterclockwise, wandering through the (mostly empty) rooms surrounding it, and imagine how the nuns once lived, secluded from the outside world. In the refectory they ate meals, copied manuscripts, and prayed many times a day. The convent was also the first hospital in Prague, known for its secret healing elixir called "swallow water," which was sold to the rich and given to the poor.

Church of Christ the Salvator and Přemyslid Crypt: During Agnes' time, the convent's church became the official burial place for the ruling Přemysl family. The Přemyslid dynasty reigned for nearly five centuries (c. 850-1306). On the floor, find two burial plaques: Queen Kunigund (d. 1248), the granddaughter of the great Frederick I Barbarossa, and her husband, King Wenceslas I (d. 1253), who saved Bohemia from the Mongol hordes of Genghis Khan.

Agnes' Oratory: This humble room is where Agnes Přemysl—the daughter of the king, and one of the most sought-after women in Europe—spent her days. She rejected many powerful suitors to become a bride of Christ and Mother Superior to this convent. When Agnes died, some speculate that she was buried here. A legend says that whenever her remains are found, the Czech nation will enter a new golden age. Her feast day on November 26 coincided with the Velvet Revolution, so Agnes is regarded as the patron saint of Czech democracy.

inviting saint—a vision of how the worlds of the spirit and flesh could unite harmoniously.

Foreign Influence (Rooms J, K, L): The harmony of the Czech golden age was shattered in the 1400s by religious warfare. The Czech lands and its art were soon dominated by foreigners—as displayed in this large hall. There's some glorious stuff here (*St. George Altar,* the *Puchner Ark*), but it lacks the distinctive look of native Bohemian art.

▶ *250 Kč; open Tue-Sun 10:00-18:00, closed Mon; two blocks northeast of the Spanish Synagogue, along the river at Anežská 12; +420 224 810 628, www.ngprague.cz.*

THE NEW TOWN (NOVÉ MĚSTO)

Enough of pretty, medieval Prague—let's leap into the modern era. The New Town, with Wenceslas Square as its focal point, is today's urban Prague, characterized by bustling boulevards and interesting neighborhoods. As you cross busy Na Příkopě, you leave the medieval cuteness and souvenir shops behind, and enter a town of malls and fancy shops. The New Town is one of the best places to view Prague's remarkable Art Nouveau architecture, and to learn more about its communist past.

🎧 My Prague City Walk audio tour covers some of these sights.

▲▲▲Wenceslas Square (Václavské Náměstí)
More a broad boulevard than a square, this city landmark is named for St. Wenceslas, whose equestrian statue overlooks the square's top end. A popular gathering place, Wenceslas Square has functioned as a stage for modern Czech history.

📖 See the Wenceslas Square Walk chapter.

▲Cold War Museum
This is my choice for a Cold War sight, as it feels more authentic than the widely advertised Museum of Communism. Located inside the Jalta Hotel, it once served as a fallout shelter. Visits are by tour only. You'll see a command room, hospital room, spying room (showing you how an operator tapped telephone conversations), and an air-filtering facility. Details such as the cheap period plastic floors are truthfully

re-created. The enthusiastic guides are a great source of information on the whole era.

▸ *400 Kč for one-hour guided tour in English, tours daily at 11:00, 13:00, 14:30, and 16:00 from inside the Jalta Hotel; book online or inquire at reception, more departures in high season, www.en.muzeum-studene-valky.cz.*

▲Mucha Museum (Muchovo Museum)

This enjoyable little museum features a small selection of the insistently likeable art of Alphonse Mucha (MOO-kah, 1860-1939), whose florid style helped define what became known as Art Nouveau. It's all crammed into a too-small space, some of the art is faded, and the admission price is steep—but there's no better place to gain an understanding of Mucha's influence on the world art scene.

📖 See the Mucha Museum Tour chapter.

▲Museum of Communism (Muzeum Komunismu)

This small museum offers a fascinating look at the "dream, reality, and nightmare" of communism. Toward the end of World War II, the Soviets "liberated" Czechoslovakia from the Nazis. The communists quickly came to power, with statues of Stalin and propaganda permeating Czech society. Along with that came cosmonaut heartthrobs, socialist heroes, collectivization of agriculture, and the focus on very heavy industry.

You'll walk through the years (with good English descriptions), from the 1918 birth of Czechoslovakia to the 1938 Munich Agreement that gave the country's Sudetenland region to Hitler.

A slice-of-life exhibit re-creates a student's bedroom in the 1960s. Then comes the dark side: attempted escapes, police, interrogation, and torture—a video on the wall shows mesmerizingly sad images, humanizing the tragedy of this period. In the school room you'll learn how "we teach Russian not English to honor the liberators of our country and our role model."

After gazing at a factory workshop and a dreary general store, you can see how, in 1980, because the law of supply and demand was ignored, the nation ran out of toilet paper. People then started using the newspaper (the voice of the Communist Party)—because it was "the best quality paper and it was never sold out."

The Museum of Communism includes an inspiring section on the fall of communism.

Stairs lead to a café, gift shop, and temporary exhibits on the top floor (your ticket comes with a free cup of coffee to lure you up there).

A section on the fall of communism is inspiring. You'll see the uprising of 1968 and learn of the "living torches" as students burned themselves alive in protest, and the Soviet crackdown that followed. With the fall of the Berlin Wall in 1989 came the Velvet Revolution, bringing freedom to Czechoslovakia and the people of Prague.

A little theater provides a powerful video finale showing the Czech people confronting the state and police in 1968 and 1989, eventually winning freedom. The video's poetic text reads like a prayer for peace and freedom.

▶ *380 Kč, daily 9:00-20:00, a block off Republic Square at V Celnici 4, +420 224 212 966, www.museumofcommunism.com.*

▲▲Municipal House (Obecní Dům)

The cultural and artistic leaders who financed this Art Nouveau masterpiece (1905-1911) wanted a ceremonial palace to reinforce self-awareness of the Czech nation. While the exterior is impressive, the highlight is the interior—and at least part of it is free. For more about the exterior, see page 29 of the 📖 Old Town & Charles Bridge Walk chapter.

Don't be timid about poking around the interior, which is open to the public. Enter under the green, wrought-iron arcade. In the **rotunda,** admire the mosaic floor, stained glass, woodwork doorway, and lighting fixtures. To the left is a recommended **café** (*kavárna*)—a harmony of woodwork, marble, metal, and glittering chandeliers.

From the rotunda, step into the **lobby,** where you can look up the staircase that leads to the main concert hall (no tourist access upstairs). Also in the lobby is the box office, selling concert tickets and guided English tours of the building.

Head **downstairs**—yes, tourists are welcome there. Admire the colorful tiles in the stairwell, and more colorful tiles in the downstairs main room. Also check out the **American Bar** (salute the US flags above the bar) and the **Plzeňská Restaurant** (with its dark-wood booths and colorful tile scenes of happy peasants).

Finish your tour by going back upstairs to find the **Modernista shop** (tucked to the left as you face the main staircase), full of fancy teacups and jewelry.

Some of the Municipal House's rich Art Nouveau rooms are free to wander.

SIGHTS

Standing sternly next to the Municipal House is the medieval **Powder Tower**—see page 28.

▶ *The entrance halls and public spaces are free (daily 10:00-18:00). For an in-depth look at all the sumptuous halls and banquet rooms, join a one-hour **tour** (290 Kč, English tours—usually 3/day departing between 11:00 and 17:00; limited to 35 people—buy your ticket online or from the ground-floor shop where tours depart; Náměstí Republiky 5, +420 222 002 101, www.obecnidum.cz).*

Prague's Islands

From the National Theater, the Bridge of Legions (Most Legií) leads across the Vltava River and the island called **Střelecký Ostrov.** Covered with chestnut trees, this island boasts Prague's best beach (on the sandy tip that points north to Charles Bridge). Bring a swimsuit and take a dip just a stone's throw from Europe's most beloved bridge.

In the mood for boating instead of swimming? On the next island up, **Slovanský Ostrov,** you can rent a rowboat or paddleboat (250-300 Kč/hour, daily 11:00-22:00, bring picture ID as deposit).

▲▲Welcome to Prague Self-Guided Tram Tour

A trip on tram #22 (or #23, using a 1960s-vintage car on the same route) is a fun way to lace together a few sights from the New Town to Prague Castle. It runs roughly every 5-10 minutes, and you can hop on and off as you like (40 Kč standard ticket valid for 1.5 hours). Be warned: Thieves and plainclothes ticket-checkers like this route as much as the tourists.

Catch the tram at Národní Třída (next to the Metro station of the

National Theater and bridge over the Vltava

Rent rowboats on nearby Slovanský Ostrov.

same name). Sit in front on the right so you can see each stop's name out your window. These are the stops along the way:

Národní Třída: Start here on the same side of Spálená street as the iconic Máj department store.

Národní Divadlo: The National Theater is on your left and the venerable old Slavia café is on the right. This is the last stop before crossing the Vltava River. You're near the boat-rental scene and the romantic beach island.

Újezd: The tram turns at Petřín Park. At the corner (on the left) leading down from the park is the Monument to Victims of Communism—with bronze figures descending the steps. Nearby, a funicular leads to the Eiffel-like Petřín Tower.

Hellichova: The tram now heads north, paralleling Kampa Island on the river side and passing the Church of Our Lady Victorious (on the left), popular with pilgrims for its Infant Jesus of Prague. The tram makes a little bump uphill, stopping in the Lesser Town.

Malostranské Náměstí: This is the closest stop to the Charles Bridge, on the Lesser Town's main square, which is dominated by the Church of St. Nicholas. From here you can hike up Nerudova street to Prague Castle. Next, you pass the Czech parliament and government buildings on the left.

Malostranská: On the left is the entry to the Wallenstein Palace Garden. On the right, a bridge leads across the Vltava River to the Neo-Renaissance Rudolfinum concert hall and the Jewish Quarter. From this stop it's a pleasant stroll down to the riverbank for great Charles Bridge views.

The tram now climbs uphill, entering a park-like zone outside the castle walls.

Královský Letohrádek: Immediately across the street on the left is the Royal Summer Palace and its entrance/security gate, the Royal Gardens leading fragrantly to Prague Castle, and a public WC. This is the place to enter Prague Castle the scenic way. ▢ See the Prague Castle Tour chapter.

Pražský Hrad: This stop is closest to the recommended northern Prague Castle entrance. Climbing higher yet, you'll see Petřín Hill and its tower on the left.

Brusnice: From here you can explore the Nový Svět (New World) neighborhood, a time capsule of cobblestone streets and tiny houses with no shops or tourists. The tram now winds through a greenbelt built along the remains of the city wall.

Pohořelec: This is the stop closest to the Strahov Monastery. Hop out here, next to the statues of astronomers Tycho Brahe and Johannes Kepler, and it's all downhill to the monastery and the castle. Or catch a tram going the opposite direction to do this trip in reverse.

Dancing House (Tančící Dům)

If ever a building could get your toes tapping, it would be this one, nicknamed "Fred and Ginger" by American architecture buffs. Located about 10 minutes south of the National Theater, this metallic samba is the work of Frank Gehry (who designed the striking Guggenheim Museum in Bilbao, Spain). Some Czechs prefer to think that the two "figures" represent the nation's greatest 20th-century heroes, Jozef Gabčík and Jan Kubiš (described next).

Eating: The building's top-floor restaurant, **$$$ Ginger and Fred,** is a fine place for a fancy meal, whether you go up for breakfast (from 7:00), a reasonably priced lunch, or an expensive dinner (daily, +420 601 158 828, www.gfrest.cz).

▲National Memorial to the Heroes of the Heydrich Terror (Národní Památník Hrdinů Heydrichiády)

This World War II-era memorial, located in the crypt of the Sts. Cyril and Methodius Church, honors the Czech resistance movement against Nazi oppression.

In 1942, the Czech lands were under the thumb of German occupation. The Nazi commander was the hated Reinhard Heydrich—one of Hitler's closest cronies, second-in-command in the SS, and one of

Busts of the heroes of the Heydrich Terror

Dancing House, by the American Frank Gehry

the architects of the Holocaust. When Heydrich took over Bohemian lands, resistance seemed futile.

But two Czech paratroopers—Jozef Gabčík and Jan Kubiš—signed up for a potentially suicidal mission to take down Heydrich. On the morning of May 27, the two men ambushed Heydrich in his car, in northern Prague. Gabčík fired first, but the gun jammed. Kubiš threw a handmade grenade that wounded Heydrich enough that he died days later. Hitler was outraged and ordered vengeance. Two Czech villages were summarily razed to the ground, and 5,000 were executed. Gabčík and Kubiš fled with a price on their heads and found refuge here in this Greek Orthodox Church. Eventually they were ratted out. On June 18, at 4:15 in the morning, the Gestapo stormed in, and a two-hour battle ensued. Kubiš was gunned down in the nave of the church. Gabčík committed suicide in the crypt.

Today, a modest exhibition in the crypt retells the story of Czech resistance. Back outside, notice the small memorial, including bullet holes, plaque, and flowers on the street. Around the corner is the entry to the museum and crypt.

▶ *Free, Tue-Sun 9:00-17:00, closed Mon, full history explained in small 25 Kč booklet, two blocks up from the Dancing House at Resslova 9A, +420 222 540 718.*

THE LESSER TOWN (MALÁ STRANA)

Huddled under the castle on the west bank of the river, just over the Charles Bridge, the Lesser Town is a Baroque time capsule. It's the oldest of the four towns that make up Prague, dating to the early 10th century. In 1540, a fire burned 75 percent of the Lesser Town. But it rose from the ashes, rebuilt by Italians to become a town of fine palaces and gardens. If you like hidden, quiet alleyways, you'll want to explore the neighborhood. From the end of the Charles Bridge, Mostecká street leads two blocks up to the Lesser Town Square and the huge Church of St. Nicholas.

Lesser Town Square (Malostranské Náměstí)

This square is split into an upper and lower part by the domineering Church of St. Nicholas. A Baroque plague column oversees the upper square (and a handy Via Musica ticket office is on the uphill side).

At the bottom of the square, the dark-gray-and-white Renaissance building was once the Lesser Town's city hall. As you face this building, note the three houses along the left side of the square. These belonged to prominent noble families involved in the 1618 uprising against the Habsburgs. Trams trundle both directions here, conveniently connecting this spot with the castle (left) and the Old and New Towns (right).

Church of St. Nicholas (Kostel Sv. Mikuláše)

When the Jesuits came to Prague, they found the perfect piece of real estate for their church—right on the Lesser Town Square. The church (built 1703-1760) is the best example of High Baroque in town. Its interior is giddy with curves and illusions. This is "dynamic Baroque," with circles intersecting circles, creating an illusion of movement. Climb the staircase in the left transept up to the **gallery** for a close-up look at large canvases and illusionary frescoes by Karel Škréta, who is considered the greatest Czech Baroque painter. And for a good look at the city and the church's 250-foot dome, climb the 215 steps up the bell tower.

▶ *Church—100 Kč, daily 9:00-18:00, Nov-Feb until 16:00; tower climb—100 Kč, daily 10:00-22:00, shorter hours in winter; tower entrance is outside the right transept.*

Sights near Lesser Town Square

A couple of sights lie between Lesser Town Square and the Charles Bridge: The **Lennon Wall** (Lennonova Zeď)—named for Beatle John Lennon—is covered with colorful graffiti. Since 1980, the wall has been a symbol of free expression. While the ideas of V. I. Lenin collapsed in 1989, the hopeful message of J. W. Lennon lives on. **Kampa Island** is a colorful neighborhood of relaxing pubs, a breezy park, hippies, lovers, a fine contemporary art gallery (Museum Kampa), and river access.

A 10-minute walk north of the square (near the Malostranská Metro station) is the entrance to the **Wallenstein Palace Garden** (Valdštejnská Palac Zahrada). Of the neighborhood's many impressive palace gardens open to the public, this is by far the biggest and most beautiful, with a large pool, Greek-style statues, amphitheater, and fake grotto (free, Mon-Fri 7:30-18:00, Sat-Sun from 10:00, daily until 19:00 in summer, closed in winter).

Kampa Island's easygoing rustic ambience   Wallenstein Palace Garden's elegance

A 5-minute walk south of the square is the **Church of Our Lady Victorious** (Kostel Panny Marie Vítězné), which displays Prague's most-worshipped treasure, the small statue of the Infant Jesus of Prague. Christians from across the globe (especially South America) make the pilgrimage to Prague just to kneel before this humble baby (free, Mon-Sat 9:30-17:30, Sun 13:00-18:00, Karmelitská 9, www.pragjesu.cz).

▲Petřín Hill (Petřínské Sady)

This hill, topped by a replica of the Eiffel Tower, features several unusual sights.

Monument to Victims of Communism (Pomník Obětem Komunismu): The sculptural figures of this poignant memorial, representing victims of the totalitarian regime, gradually atrophy as they range up the hillside steps. The statistics inscribed on the steps say it all: From 1948 until 1989, in Czechoslovakia alone, 205,486 people were imprisoned, 248 were executed, 4,500 died in prison, 327 were shot attempting to cross the border, and 170,938 left the country.

Hunger Wall (Hladová Zeď'): To the left of the monument is this medieval defense wall, which was Charles IV's 14th-century work-for-food project. The poorest of the poor helped build this structure just to eke out a bit of income.

To the right (about 50 yards away) is the base of a handy **funicular** you can ride up the hill to the Petřín Tower (uses tram/Metro ticket, runs daily every 10-15 minutes 8:00-22:00).

Petřín Hill Summit and Tower: The top of Petřín Hill is considered the best place in Prague to take your date for a romantic city view. Built for an exhibition in 1891, the 200-foot-tall Petřín Tower is one-fifth the height of its Parisian big brother, built two years earlier. Before you climb up, appreciate the tower's sinuous curves. Climbing the 400 steps rewards you with amazing views of the city (150 Kč, daily 9:00-21:00, shorter hours off-season). Czech couples come to the orchard-filled slope of Petřín Hill each May Day to reaffirm their love with a kiss under a blooming sour-cherry tree.

THE CASTLE QUARTER (HRADČANY)

Looming above Prague, dominating its skyline, is the Castle Quarter. Prague Castle and its surrounding sights are packed with Czech history, as well as tourists. This vast and sprawling complex has been the seat of Czech power for centuries. It collects a wide range of sights, including the country's top church, its former royal palace, and an assortment of history and art museums. Most of these sights, including an in-depth tour of St. Vitus Cathedral, are covered in far greater detail in the ▭ Prague Castle Tour chapter. You'll also find crowd-beating tips and a recommended route for connecting the sights. If taking the tram to the castle, see my "Welcome to Prague Self-Guided Tram Tour," earlier.

Castle Square (Hradčanské Náměstí) and Ticket Offices

At the main entrance to the castle, this square is ringed by important buildings and art galleries. A statue of the statesman Tomáš Garrigue Masaryk (who led Czechoslovakia after World War I) surveys the scene. Above the gilded gateway to the complex, stone giants battle, while real-life soldiers stand stiffly at attention...until the ceremonial changing of the guard at the top of each hour.

▭ See page 105 of the Prague Castle Tour chapter.

▲▲▲St. Vitus Cathedral (Katedrála Sv. Víta)

This towering house of worship—with its flying buttresses and spiny spires—is the top church of the Czech people. Many VIPs from this nation's history, from saints to statesmen, are buried here—including the most important Czech saint, St. Wenceslas.

For a self-guided tour of the cathedral, see the ▭ Prague Castle Tour chapter.

▲▲Lobkowicz Palace

Located below the Golden Lane medieval merchant street, this palace exhibits a Czech noble family's private collection, with some top-notch paintings, ceramics, a Beethoven manuscript, and Mozart's handwritten reworking of Handel's "Messiah" on display.

📖 See page 103 of the Prague Castle Tour chapter.

▲Strahov Monastery and Library
(Strahovský Klášter a Knihovna)

This fine old monastery has sat perched on the hill just above Prague Castle since the 12th century. If you'd like to combine the monastery with your castle visit, it's easy to ride Tram #22/23 up to the Pohořelec stop (beyond the castle), visit the monastery, then walk 10 minutes down to Castle Square—passing Loreta Church on the way.

Medieval monasteries such as this one were a mix of industry, agriculture, and education, as well as worship and theology. In its heyday, Strahov Monastery had a booming economy of its own, with vineyards, a brewery, and a sizable beer hall—all now open once again.

The monastery's **main church** was decorated by the monks in textbook Baroque (usually closed, but look through the gate inside the front door to see its interior). Go ahead, inhale: That's the scent of Baroque.

The **library** is just to the right of the church—head up the stairs for a peek at how enlightened thinkers in the 18th century influenced learning. The **display cases** in the library gift shop show off illuminated manuscripts, described in English. The theme of the first and bigger hall is **philosophy,** with the history of the Western pursuit of knowledge painted on the ceiling. The second hall—down a hallway lined with antique furniture—focuses on **theology.** Notice the gilded, locked case containing the *libri prohibiti* (prohibited books) at the end of the room, above the mirror. Only the abbot had the key.

▶ *Grounds—free and always open; library—150 Kč, daily 9:00-12:00 & 13:00-17:00, +420 233 107 718, www.strahovskyklaster.cz.*

Sights near the Monastery

Outside, in front of the monastery, that hoppy smell you're enjoying is the recommended **Klášterní Pivovar,** where they brew beer just

The Strahov Monastery library has a painted ceiling and a locked case of (once) prohibited books.

as monks have for centuries (in the little courtyard across from the library entrance; open daily). Don't miss the monastery's **garden terrace** with exquisite views over the domes and spires of Prague.

▲Loreta Church

This church has been a hit with pilgrims for centuries, thanks to its dazzling bell tower, peaceful yet plush cloister, sparkling treasury, and much-venerated Holy House.

In the garden-like center of the cloister stands the ornate **Santa Casa (Holy House),** considered by some pilgrims to be part of Mary's home in Nazareth (including an original beam). The Santa Casa might seem like a bit of a letdown, but generations of believers have considered this to be the holiest spot in the country.

The small **Baroque church** is one of the most beautiful in Prague. The decor looks rich, but the marble and gold are all fake. In the cloister's last corner, on the left wall of the chapel, is **"St. Bearded Woman"** (Svatá Starosta). This patron saint of unhappy marriages prayed for an escape from an arranged marriage and sprouted a beard...and the guy said, "No way." The many candles here are from people suffering through uncivil unions.

Upstairs, the **treasury** is full of jeweled worship aids (well described in English). The highlight is a monstrance (Communion-wafer holder) from 1699, with more than 6,000 diamonds.

Enjoy the short **carillon concert** at the top of the hour in front of the main entrance

▸ *210 Kč; daily 9:00-17:00, Nov-March 9:30-16:00; audioguide-150 Kč, +420 220 516 740, www.loreta.cz.*

OUTSIDE THE CENTER

▲Vyšehrad

If you're looking to escape the tourists—while digging more deeply into Czech culture and history (and enjoying fine city views)—head for the hilltop fortress-turned-park called Vyšehrad (VEE-sheh-rahd), just south of the center. While there, ogle the dynamic statues of Bohemian folkloric figures and dip into the National Cemetery to pay your respects to Czech greats such as Mucha and Dvořák.

The walled town of Terezín, which Nazis made a concentration camp, houses a poignant memorial.

▶ *The park is free and open all the time (though the church closes at 18:00 and the cemetery closes between 17:00 and 19:00). To get there, ride the Metro to the Vyšehrad stop and hike five minutes downhill.*

▲▲Day Trips from Prague

Travelers find a wide range of interesting one-day side trips from Prague. **Kutná Hora** is a workaday Czech town with an offbeat bone church, stunning cathedral, and silver mining museum. **Terezín,** where the Nazis created the notorious Theresienstadt Jewish ghetto and transit/concentration camp, is now a sobering memorial. **Karlovy Vary** (Carlsbad) is a well-known and swanky spa town.

In addition, three castles compete for your attention: **Konopiště Castle** is the opulent but lived-in former residence of the Archduke Franz Ferdinand. **Karlštejn Castle** is historic and dramatically situated. **Křivoklát Castle** is a genuinely Gothic hunting palace.

You can do these on your own by public transportation or a rental car. Otherwise, try a guided day trip with Premiant City Tours (www.premiant.cz), Wittmann Tours (www.wittmann-tours.com), or a private guide (see my recommendations on page 132).

Activities

Castles and museums are nice, but there's plenty more to see and do in Prague. In this chapter you'll find suggestions for tours, shopping, and a variety of very Czech evening entertainment. Take a walking tour for further insight—whether serious or humorous—into this great city. Shopping for authentic Czech souvenirs (puppets, crystal, and Art Nouveau design) is a cultural experience in itself. And for nightlife, there's no place like Prague for a classical music performance or the entertaining absurdity of Black Light Theater—this city's specialty.

Walking Tours

A staggering number of small companies offer walking tours of the Old Town, the castle, and more (check at the TI). You'll generally get hardworking young guides with fine language skills at good prices. The quality depends on the guide rather than the company. Your best bet is to show up at the Astronomical Clock a couple of minutes before 8:00, 10:00, or 11:00, then chat with a few of the umbrella-holding guides. Choose the one you click with.

As for the "free" tours you may see, they are not really free—you're expected to tip your guide (with bills, not coins) when finished. The guides are usually expat students who memorize a script and give an entertaining performance as you walk through the Old Town, with little respect for serious history.

Local Guides

In Prague, hiring a guide is particularly smart (and a ▲▲ experience). Expect to pay around 3,000 Kč for a half-day tour. Because prices are usually per hour, small groups can hire an inexpensive guide for a

"Free" walking tours indicate a trend—it's a buyer's market (but expect to tip).

whole day or for chunks of time over several days. Guides meet you wherever you like and tailor the tour to your interests.

Guide Services: These two outfits represent a cadre of top-notch guides.

At **PragueWalker,** Kateřina Svobodová, a hardworking historian-guide, manages a team of enthusiastic and friendly guides (+420 603 181 300, www.praguewalker.com, katerina@praguewalker.com).

At **Personal Prague Guide Service,** Šárka Kačabová uses her teaching background to help you understand Czech culture and has a team of personable and knowledgeable guides (RS%—30 minutes free with this book, +420 777 225 205, www.personalpragueguide.com).

Private Guides: These guides generally learned their trade post-communism but can still share memories of the time before the transition. For even more guides, see www.guide-prague.cz.

Jana Hronková has a natural style—a welcome change from the more strict professionalism of some other guides—and a penchant for the Jewish Quarter (+420 732 185 180, https://praguediscoveries.com). A tour with my co-author, **Honza Vihan,** adds more nuance and context to the history covered in this guidebook (+420 603 418 148, honzavihan@hotmail.com). **Zuzana Tlášková** speaks Hebrew in addition to English (+420 774 131 335, tlaskovaz@seznam.cz). **Martin Bělohradský,** formerly an organic-chemistry professor, is enthusiastic about fine arts and architecture (+420 723 414 565, martinb5666@gmail.com).

Jana Krátká enjoys sharing Prague's tumultuous 20th-century history with visitors (+420 776 571 538, janapragueguide@gmail.com). Friendly **Petra Vondroušová** designs tours to fit your interests (+420 602 319 420, www.compactprague.com). **Kamil and Pavlína** run a family business specializing in tours of Prague and beyond. They also provide sightseeing and transport as far as Vienna and Berlin (+420 605 701 861, https://prague-extra.com).

Jewish Quarter Tours

Jewish guides (of varying quality) lead private three-hour tours in English of the Jewish Quarter. Consider **Wittmann Tours** (4,800 Kč, or 6,800 Kč with Sylvie Wittman herself, plus museum entry fees; +420 603 426 564, www.wittmann-tours.com).

Bus Tours

Since Prague's sightseeing core (Castle Quarter, Charles Bridge, and the Old Town) is not accessible by bus, I don't recommend any of the city's bus-tour companies. Prague—so delightful on foot—doesn't lend itself to the **hop-on, hop-off bus-tour** formula. But, bus tours can make sense for day trips out of Prague. Several companies have kiosks on Na Příkopě, where you can comparison-shop. **Premiant City Tours'** many offerings include a tour to Český Krumlov or Karlovy Vary (+420 606 600 123, www.premiant.cz). **Wittmann Tours,** listed earlier under "Jewish Quarter Tours," offers an all-day minibus tour to the Terezín Memorial.

Food Tours

If you would like to delve more deeply into Czech food or beer, consider **Eating Europe**'s culinary and beer tours (www.eatingeurope.com).

SHOPPING

Prague's entire Old Town seems designed to bring out the shopper in visitors. Puppets, glass, crystal, and garnet gemstones are traditional; fashion and design (especially incorporating the city's rich Art Nouveau heritage) are also big business.

Most shops are open on weekdays 9:00-17:00 or 18:00—and often longer, especially for tourist-oriented shops. Some close on Saturday afternoons and/or all day Sunday.

For easy shopping in the tourist zone, consider the following streets. (Keep in mind that any shop in the city center caters primarily to tourists—most locals do their shopping in the suburbs.)

The Ungelt, the courtyard tucked behind the Týn Church just off of the Old Town Square, is packed with touristy but decent-quality shops.

Michalská, a semihidden lane right in the thick of the tourist zone, has a variety of shops (from the Small Market Square/Malé Náměstí near the Astronomical Clock, go through the big stone gateway marked 459).

On **Havelská** street, you can browse the open-air Havelská Market, a touristy but enjoyable place to shop for inexpensive

The Ungelt courtyard offers convenient (and decent) shopping in the tourist zone.

handicrafts and fresh produce (daily 9:00-18:00, two long blocks south of the Old Town Square).

Celetná, exiting the Old Town Square to the right of Týn Church, is lined with big stores selling all the traditional Czech goodies. Tourists wander endlessly here, mesmerized by the window displays.

Na Příkopě, following the former moat between the Old Town and the New Town, has the city center's handiest lineup of modern shopping malls. The best is **Slovanský Dům** ("Slavic House," at #22), with classy restaurants and designer shops surrounding a peaceful courtyard. Na Příkopě street opens up into Republic Square (Náměstí Republiky)—boasting Prague's biggest mall, **Palladium,** hidden behind a pink Neo-Romanesque facade. Across the square is the communist-era brown steel-and-glass 1980s department store **Kotva** ("Anchor"), which has been recently remodeled inside.

Národní Třída (National Street), which continues past Na Příkopě in the opposite direction (toward the river), is less touristy and lined with some inviting stores. The big **Tesco** department store in the middle (at #26) sells anything you might need (long hours daily).

Karlova, the tourist-clogged drag connecting the Old Town Square to the Charles Bridge, should be avoided entirely. Shops along here sell made-in-China trinkets at too-high prices.

Souvenirs

Czech Puppets: Czechs have treasured the art of puppets for centuries; at times of heavy German influence in the 18th century, traveling puppet troupes kept the Czech language and humor alive in the countryside. Czech grandfathers bequeathed to their grandsons their linden wood-carved designs. It takes a rare artist to turn pieces of wood into nimble (and pricey) puppets, but even a simple jester, witch, or Pinocchio can make a thoughtful memento. A higher-quality keepsake starts at around $100. Try **Galerie Michael** (U Lužického Semináře 7, www.buymarionettes.com) or the **Loutky** ("Puppets") shop (at the top of Nerudova, at #51, www.loutky.cz). Closer to the Old Town Square, check out **Hračky, Loutky** ("Toys, Puppets") in the Ungelt courtyard.

Glass and Crystal: Since the Renaissance, Prague has been known for its exquisite glass and crystal. Legally, to be called "crystal" (or "lead crystal"), it must contain at least 24 percent lead oxide, which gives it that prismatic sparkle. The lead also adds weight, makes the glass easier to cut, and produces a harmonious ringing when flicked. ("Crystal glass" has a smaller percentage of lead.) **Moser** is the most famous and expensive Czech brand, with a flagship store at the Černá Růže shopping mall at Na Příkopě 12 (and shops all over Prague, www.moser.com). **Blue** specializes in sleek, modern designs (several shops near the Old Town Square at Malé Náměstí 13, Pařížská 3, Melantrichova 6, and Celetná 2; one near the Lesser Town end of the Charles Bridge at Mostecká 24; and at the airport, www.bluepraha. cz). **Celetná street** is lined with touristy glass shops selling a variety of crystal items.

Bohemian Garnets (*Granát*): These blood-colored gemstones have unique refractive properties. Much of the authentic Bohemian garnet jewelry you'll see today is Victorian-era—these traditional hand-crafted designs pack many small garnets together on one piece. Ask for a certificate of authenticity to avoid buying a glass imitation (these are common). A *"granát Turnov"* label is a good indicator of quality. Of the many garnet shops, **Turnov Granát Co-op** has the

Puppets—both artistic and traditional

Havelská Market—gifts and people-watching

largest selection (shops at Dlouhá 28, Panská 1, and inside the Pánská Pasáž at Na Příkopě 23; www.granat.cz). **J. Drahoňovský's Studio Šperk** is an upscale-feeling shop with more creative designs (Dlouhá 19, www.drahonovsky.cz). Additional shops specializing in Turnov garnets are at Dlouhá 1, Celetná 8, and Maiselova 3.

Costume Jewelry and Beads: You'll see *bižutérie* (costume jewelry) all over town. Round, glass beads—also called Druk beads—are popular and range in size. Jablonex is the biggest producer. **Material,** in the Ungelt courtyard, has a fun selection (www.i-material.com).

Art Nouveau Design: Prague is Europe's best Art Nouveau city— and several shops sell that eye-pleasing style in the form of glassware, home decor, linens, posters, and other items. Browse **Artěl,** which specializes in glass with Art Nouveau, Art Deco, and floral motifs (by Lesser Town end of Charles Bridge at U Lužického Semináře 7; www.artelglass.com); **Modernista,** with a good selection of Art Nouveau and Art Deco jewelry, glassware, wooden toys, books, and so on (Municipal House, www.modernista.cz); and **Kubista,** in the House of the Black Madonna, with Czech Cubist dishes, jewelry, furniture, books, and more (closed Mon, Ovocný Trh 19, www.kubista.cz).

Other Fun Souvenirs: Look for old-fashioned porcelain (traditional blue design on a white base), stuffed animal and other depictions of cartoon character Krtek, the brain-teasing puzzle "hedgehog in the cage" (*ježek v kleci*), the "fishlet" (sardine-shaped pocketknife), and "kitchen witch" good-luck dolls.

Buyer Beware: Many souvenir shops sell very non-Czech (often Russian) items, such as stacking dolls, fur hats, vodka flasks, and amber, which is found along the Baltic Sea coast and is mostly Russian and Polish.

VAT and Customs

Getting a VAT Refund: If you purchase more than 2,001 Kč worth of goods at a single store, you may be eligible to get a refund of the 21 percent Value-Added Tax (VAT). Get more details from your merchant or see RickSteves.com/vat.

Customs for American Shoppers: You can take home $800 worth of items per person duty-free, once every 31 days. You can bring in one liter of alcohol duty-free. For details on allowable goods, customs rules, and duty rates, visit Help.CBP.gov.

ENTERTAINMENT

Prague booms with live and inexpensive theater, classical music, jazz, and pop entertainment. Everything is listed in several monthly cultural events programs (free at TIs). To understand your options, drop by the **Via Musica** box office—next to Týn Church on the Old Town Square (daily 10:00-20:00, +420 224 826 440, www.viamusica.cz) or the **Time Music** shop in Lesser Town Square across from the Church of St. Nicholas (daily 10:00-20:00, +420 257 535 568). Locals dress up for the more serious concerts, opera, and ballet, but many tourists wear casual clothes (avoid shorts, sneakers, or flip-flops).

Black Light Theater

A kind of mime/modern dance variety show, Black Light Theater has no language barrier. Unique to Prague, it originated in the 1960s as a playful and mystifying theater of the absurd. Shows last about an hour and a half—avoid the first two rows, which are too close and can ruin the illusion. Each of these theaters has its own spin on Black Light:

Black Light Theatre Srnec: Run by Jiří Srnec, who invented the Black Light Theater concept in 1961, this troupe offers simple narratives and revels in the childlike, goofy wonder of the effects (generally nightly, on Národní Třída in the same building as the Reduta Jazz Club, Národní 20, +420 774 574 475, www.srnectheatre.com).

Image Theater: This slapsticky show has more mime and elements of the absurd, and more dance along with the illusions (nightly, off Národní Třída 25 in the Metro passageway, +420 222 314 448, www.imagetheatre.cz).

Go to a Black Light Theater show for an absurdly Prague experience.

Classical Concerts

Each day, six to eight classical concerts designed for tourists fill delightful Old World halls and churches with crowd-pleasing music: Vivaldi, Best of Mozart, Most Famous Arias, and works by the famous Czech composer Antonín Dvořák. Concerts typically cost 400-1,000 Kč, start anywhere from 13:00 to 21:00, and last about an hour.

For a memorable concert, see one at Smetana Hall, the Rudolfinum, or the National Theater. These orchestras perform in their home venues about five nights a month from September through June: The **Prague Symphony Orchestra** plays mainly in the gorgeous Art Nouveau Smetana Hall of the Municipal House. Their ticket office is inside the building, just to the left past the main entrance (Mon-Fri 10:00-18:00, +420 222 002 336, www.fok.cz). The **Czech Philharmonic** performs in the classical Neo-Renaissance Rudolfinum. Their ticket office is on the right side of the building, under the stairs (Mon-Fri 10:00-18:00, and until just before showtime on concert days, on Palachovo Náměstí on the Old Town side of Mánes

Bridge, +420 227 059 227, www.ceskafilharmonie.cz). On most other nights these spaces are rented to agencies that organize tourist concerts of varying quality.

Opera and Ballet

A handy ticket office for the following theaters (all part of the National Theater group) is directly across the street from the main entrance to the Estates Theater on Železná street.

The **National Theater** (Národní Divadlo) has a stunning Neo-Renaissance interior to match its status as the top venue in the country (+420 224 901 448, www.narodni-divadlo.cz). The **Estates Theater** (Stavovské Divadlo) is where Mozart premiered and directed many of his most beloved works (on a square called Ovocný Trh, +420 224 901 448, www.narodni-divadlo.cz). The **State Opera** (Státní Opera) typically has ballets and operas by non-Czech composers (4 Wilsonova, between the main train station and Wenceslas Square, +420 224 901 448, www.narodni-divadlo.cz).

The National Theater is the top spot to enjoy classical music, opera, and ballet.

Top-notch classical music is everywhere.

Groove to classic jazz at the Reduta Jazz Club.

Music Clubs

Young locals keep Prague's many music clubs in business. Most clubs are neighborhood institutions, generally holding only 100-200 people. You'll find live rock, Bob Dylan-style folk, and jazz clubs. Here are some good options:

Roxy, near the Old Town Square, features live bands twice a week—anything from Irish punk to Balkan brass—and experimental DJs spinning a healthy dose of Japanese pop (Dlouhá 33, www.roxy.cz). **Agharta Jazz Club** showcases some of the best Czech and Eastern European jazz just off the Old Town Square in a cool Gothic cellar (Železná 16, +420 222 211 275, www.agharta.cz). **Lucerna Music Bar,** on Wenceslas Square, is popular for its '80s and '90s video parties on Friday and Saturday nights (in the basement of Lucerna Arcade, Vodičkova 36, +420 224 217 108, www.musicbar.cz). The small **Reduta Jazz Club** launches you into the 1960s-era classic jazz scene with regular performances by top Czech jazzmen Stivín and Koubková (on Národní Třída next to Café Louvre, +420 224 933 487, www.redutajazzclub.cz). **Malostranská Beseda,** in the Lesser Town, is a tight, standing-room-only space with daily live performances (Malostranské Náměstí 21, +420 776 381 850 www.malostranska-beseda.cz).

Sleeping

I've grouped my hotel listings into four neighborhoods: the **Old Town** (central and atmospheric but more expensive), the **Lesser Town** (quiet and quaint, walking distance to Old Town and castle), **New Town** (better value, less-touristed, walk or short tram ride to center), and **Away from the Center** (best value, longer tram ride to center).

I like hotels that are clean, central, reasonably priced, friendly, small enough to have a hands-on owner and stable staff, and run with a respect for Czech traditions. I've also included a few pensions (bed-and-breakfasts) and hostels (beds in a dorm room and a few doubles).

Book as far in advance as possible, especially for May, June, September, Easter, and New Year's.

Prague Hotels

Plan on Western European-level prices ($100-200 per double). Some hotels can add an extra bed (for a small charge) to turn a double into a triple; some offer larger rooms for four or more people (I call these "family rooms").

Most hotel rooms have a TV and free Wi-Fi, which can vary in strength and quality. Simpler places rarely have a room phone. Breakfast is generally included with your room. It's sometimes continental, but often a buffet.

Making Reservations

Reserve your rooms as soon as you've pinned down your travel dates. Book your room directly by email, phone, or through the hotel's official website. The hotelier wants to know:

- Type(s) of room(s) you want and number of guests
- Number of nights you'll stay
- Arrival and departure dates, written European-style as day/month (for example, 18/06 or 18 June)
- Special requests (en suite bathroom, cheapest room, twin beds vs. double bed, quiet room)
- Applicable discounts (such as a Rick Steves discount, cash discount, or promotional rate)

Most places will request a credit-card number to hold your room. If the hotel's website doesn't have a secure form where you can enter the number directly, share this info via a phone call. If you must cancel, it's courteous—and smart—to do so with as much notice as possible. Cancellation policies can be strict; read the fine print.

Always call or email to reconfirm your reservation a few days in advance. For pensions or very small hotels, I call again on my arrival day to tell my host what time to expect me (especially important if arriving after 17:00).

Budget Tips

Comparison-shop by checking prices at several hotels (on each hotel's website, on a booking site, or by email). For the best deal, book *directly with the hotel*. Ask for a discount if paying in cash.

Sleep Code

Dollar signs reflect average rates for a standard double room with breakfast in high season.

$$$$	**Splurge:**	Most rooms over 4,000 Kč (roughly $200)
$$$	**Pricier:**	3,200-4,000 Kč ($160-200)
$$	**Moderate:**	2,300-3,200 Kč ($115-160)
$	**Budget:**	1,500-2,300 Kč ($75-115)
¢	**Backpacker:**	Under 1,500 Kč ($75)
RS%	**Rick Steves discount**	

Unless otherwise noted, credit cards are accepted and hotel staff speak basic English. If the listing includes **RS%**, request a Rick Steves discount.

A short-term rental in an apartment is a popular alternative, especially if you plan to settle in one location for several nights. You can usually find a rental that's comparable to—and cheaper than—a hotel room with similar amenities. Plus, you'll get a behind-the-scenes peek into how locals live. Websites such as Airbnb, FlipKey, Booking.com, and VRBO let you browse a wide range of properties.

A hostel provides cheap beds in dorms where you sleep alongside strangers for usually under $20 per night. Travelers of any age are welcome if they don't mind dorm-style accommodations and meeting other travelers. Most hostels offer kitchen facilities, guest computers, Wi-Fi, and a self-service laundry. Hostels almost always provide bedding, but the towel's up to you (though you can usually rent one). Family and private rooms are often available.

Sleeping just outside central Prague can save you money—and gets you away from other tourists and into more workaday residential neighborhoods.

OLD TOWN

Sights, restaurants, pubs, and ambience make this area desirable but higher priced. All my listings are within a 10-minute walk of the Old Town Square.

$$$$ Hotel Metamorphis A splurge in a former caravanserai, breakfast room in a spacious medieval cellar, some street-facing rooms noisy at night.

Malá Štupartská 5, +420 221 771 011, www.hotelmetamorphis.cz

$$$$ Hotel Maximilian Sleek, Art Deco hotel with big, plush living rooms on a perfect little square.

Haštalská 14, +420 225 303 111, www.maximilianhotel.com

$$$ Design Hotel Jewel Modern, comfortable rooms in a plain building, three blocks off the Old Town Square, RS%—use promo code "ricksteves10," no elevator.

Rytířská 3, +420 224 211 699, www.hoteljewelprague.com

$$$ The Dominican Still functional monastery with 28 luxurious, historic rooms; pleasantly intimate, breakfast extra. *Jilská 235/7, hotel entrance on Jalovcová, +420 224 248 555, www.axxoshotels.com*

$$$ Brewery Hotel u Medvídků Comfortable rooms in a big, rustic, medieval shell with dark wood furniture; beerhall noise Fri-Sat—ask for quiet room, RS%—use promo code "oldgott," apartment available.

Na Perštýně 7, +420 224 211 916, www.umedvidku.cz

$$$ Unitas Hotel Former convent and communist prison offers plush comfort and bright, airy rooms.

Bartolomějská 9, +420 224 230 533, www.unitas.cz

$$ Hotel Haštal Popular family-run hotel complements neighborhood's 1900s architecture, comfortable rooms insulated against noise, RS%, air-con.

Haštalská 16, +420 222 314 335, www.hastal.com

$$ Green Garland Pension Nine clean and simply furnished rooms in a warmly decorated 14th-century building, RS%, family room, no elevator.

Řetězová 10, +420 222 220 178, www.uzv.cz

LESSER TOWN

Quiet, cobbled-lane area near quaint restaurants and shops. Walking distance to castle or Old Town (across the Charles Bridge).

$$$$ Hotel Nerudova 211 Eight suites and two apartments in a Baroque house with painted ceilings, frescoed walls, and tile stoves; family-run.

Nerudova 14, +420 601 211 000, https://nerudova211.com

$$$$ Hotel Sax Decorated in a retro, meet-the-Jetsons fashion; distinctly modern and stylish, no-nonsense place; air-con, elevator.

Jánský Vršek 3, +420 775 859 694, www.hotelsax.cz

$$$ Hotel Julián An oasis in an untouristy neighborhood; 33 spacious, well-furnished rooms hide behind a noble Neoclassical facade; friendly staff, RS%, family rooms, air-con, elevator, roof terrace, parking.

Elišky Peškové 11, Praha 5, +420 257 311 150, www.hoteljulian.com

$$$ Dům u Velké Boty Quintessential family hotel; homey, comfy, and extremely friendly; most rooms decorated in a tasteful Biedermeier style, RS%, cash only, cheaper rooms with shared bath, family rooms, kids up to age 10 sleep free.

Vlašská 30, +420 257 532 088, www.dumuvelkeboty.cz

$$$ Mooo Apartment Spacious apartments with kitchenettes in a meticulously restored 500-year-old house, some rooms without air-con.

Jánský Vršek 8, +420 277 016 830, www.mooo-apartments.com

$$ Residence Thunovská Six rooms equipped with kitchenettes and Italian furniture, RS%, breakfast extra.

Thunovská 19, +420 721 855 880, www.thunovska19.cz

NEW TOWN

Workaday untouristed urban neighborhoods on the outer fringe of the New Town, within several minutes' walk of the sightseeing zone, well served by trams.

$$$ Hotel Cube Angular design and appealing location on quiet street just behind the National Theater, family rooms.

Křemencova 18, +420 251 019 811, www.hotelcube.cz

$$$ Mosaic House "Green" hotel with 90 rooms ranging from tiny to spacious, large but not impersonal, café, library, spa.

Odborů 4, +420 277 016 880, www.mosaichouse.com

$$ Hotel 16 Sleek and modern business-class place, Art Nouveau facade, polished cherry-wood elegance, RS%, back rooms quieter, air-con, elevator.

Kateřinská 16, +420 776 245 960, no website, adam.sneider@vfn.cz

$$ Hotel Anna Bright, simple, pastel rooms with basic service, elevator.

Budečská 17, +420 222 513 111, www.hotelanna.cz

AWAY FROM THE CENTER

Set in workaday residential neighborhoods, these listings are great values and are a short tram or Metro ride from the center.

$$$ Art Hotel Located in a prewar district packed with cafés and local flavor, 24 classy rooms, courtyard garden.

Královskou Oborou 53, +420 608 340 356, www.arthotel.cz

$$ Hotel Adalbert In historic Břevnov Monastery, caters primarily to business clientele, atmospheric pub, free parking.

Markétská 1, +420 220 406 170, www.hoteladalbert.cz

¢ Hostel Elf Fun-loving, ramshackle, and graffiti-covered; cheap, basic beds (and beer); helpful staff, private rooms available.

Husitská 11, +420 222 540 963, www.hostelelf.com

¢ Sophie's Hostel On a quiet street, modern design in an Art Nouveau building, private rooms and apartment available.

Melounova 2, +420 210 011 300, https://sophieshostel.com

Eating

A big part of Prague's charm is found in wandering aimlessly through the city's winding old quarters, sniffing out fun restaurants. You can eat well here for relatively little money. In addition to meat-and-potatoes Czech cuisine, you'll find trendy, student-oriented bars and some fine international eateries. For ambience, the options include traditional, dark Czech beer halls; elegant Art Nouveau dining rooms; and modern cafés—wonderfully rustic places with reasonably good, inexpensive food.

Generally, if you walk just a few minutes away from the tourist flow, you'll find better value, atmosphere, and service. I've listed eating and drinking establishments by neighborhood. Most of the options—and highest prices—are in the Old Town. I've also listed places in the New Town, Lesser Town, and the Castle Quarter.

When in Prague...

I eat on the Czech schedule. For breakfast, I eat at the hotel (bread, meat, cheese, cereal) or grab a pastry and coffee at a café. Lunch might be a sandwich, international takeout, a light meal in a café, or a restaurant lunch special. In the afternoon, Czechs might enjoy a coffee in an atmospheric café or a beverage with friends at an outdoor table or cozy pub. Dinner is the time for slowing down and savoring a multicourse restaurant meal, or digging into hearty fare in a traditional beer hall.

Restaurants

In general, Czech restaurants are open Sunday through Thursday 11:00-22:00, and Friday and Saturday 11:00-24:00. If they have different hours, I note it in their listings.

Only a rude waiter will rush you. Good service is relaxed (slow to an American). You can stay in a pub as long as you want—no one will bring you the *účet* (bill) until you ask for it: *"Pane vrchní, zaplatím!"* (PAH-neh VURCH-nee zah-plah-TEEM; "Mr. Waiter, now I pay!").

A Czech restaurant is a social place where people come to relax. Tables are not private. You can ask to join someone, and you'll most likely make some new friends. After a sip of beer, ask for the *jídelní lístek* (menu).

Most restaurants tack a menu onto their door for browsers and have an English menu inside. Smoking is not allowed inside restaurants and cafés, but it's generally permitted in outdoor eating areas.

Tipping: Tip only at restaurants that have table service. If you order your food at a counter, don't tip. At Czech restaurants that have a waitstaff, service is generally not included; it's common to round up the bill after a good meal (about 10 percent). If you warm up the waiter

Lunch specials can be a great deal.

Cafés and pubs also serve meals.

Restaurant Code

Dollar signs reflect the cost of a typical main course.

$$$$ **Splurge:** Most main courses over 600 Kč (roughly $30)

$$$ **Pricier:** 350-600 Kč ($15-30)

$$ **Moderate:** 200-350 Kč ($10-15)

$ **Budget:** Under 200 Kč ($10)

A pub, basic sit-down eatery, and less-touristy café or teahouse is **$**; a typical restaurant—or a fancy café—is **$$**; an upscale restaurant is **$$$**; and a swanky splurge is **$$$$**.

with a few Czech words, such as "please" (*prosím;* PROH-zeem) and "thank you" (*děkuji;* DYACK-khuyi), you'll get better service and won't be expected to tip more than a local. If paying with a credit card, be prepared to tip separately with cash or coins; credit-card receipts often don't have a tip line.

Cafés, Bars, and Pubs

Besides the full-service restaurant (*restaurace),* you can also generally get food at a pub (*hostinec)* or a bar (*hospoda).* Many cafés also serve light lunches, though some only serve coffee. Also look for takeout-food stands, bakeries (with sandwiches and small pizzas to go), delis with stools or a table, department-store cafeterias, salad bars, or simple little eateries for fast and easy sit-down food. Wherever you go, a good place to start the experience is by ordering a beer.

Beer (*Pivo):* Czechs are among the world's most enthusiastic beer drinkers—adults drink an average of 80 gallons a year. The pub is a place to have fun, complain, discuss art and politics, talk hockey, and chat with locals and visitors alike. A beer will land on your table upon the slightest hint to the waiter, and a new pint will automatically appear when the old glass is almost empty (until you tell the waiter to stop). If you simply order a *pivo,* you'll get a large draft beer (0.5 liter—17 oz); a *malé pivo* is small (0.3 liter—10 oz).

The Czechs perfected the first Pilsner-style lager in nearby Plzeň, and the result, Pilsner Urquell, is on tap in many local pubs. But the Czechs also produce Budvar, from the town of Budějovice ("Budweis" in German). For years, the Czech and the American

Czechs *lo-o-ove* beer, especially Pilsners.

Prague offers lots of meals with a view.

breweries disputed the "Budweiser" brand name. The solution: Czech Budweiser is sold under its own name in Europe, China, and Africa, while in America it is marketed as Czechvar. The big degree symbol on beer bottles doesn't indicate alcohol content. Instead, it is a measurement used by brewers to track the density of certain ingredients. The most popular Czech beers are about as potent as German beers and only slightly stronger than typical American brews.

Traditional establishments have beers from only one brewery on tap, but in more recent years the Czechs have moved toward local microbrews. More and more restaurants are making their own beer or serving beer only from independent breweries. Modern beer bars (*pivní bar*, with a range of microbrews on tap) are popping up like crazy.

Czech Cuisine

The Czechs have one of Europe's most stick-to-your-ribs cuisines. Heavy on meat, potatoes, and cabbage, it's hearty and tasty—designed to keep peasants fueled through a day of hard work.

Soups: *Polévka* (soup) is the most essential part of a meal. *Pečivo* (bread) may be served with soup, or you may need to ask for it; it's always charged separately. Some of the thick soups for a cold day are *zelná* (or *zelňačka*, cabbage), *čočková* (lentil), *fazolová* (bean), and *dršťková* (tripe). The lighter soups are *hovězí* (beef or chicken broth with noodles), *pórková* (leek), and *květáková* (cauliflower).

Main Dishes: Here are some popular meat dishes; note that the word *pečené* (roasted) shows up frequently on menus: *guláš* (thick, meaty stew), *pečená kachna* (roasted duck), *pečené kuře* (roasted chicken), *smažený řízek* (fried pork fillet), *svíčková na smetaně* (beef tenderloin in cream sauce), *vepřové koleno* (pork knuckle), and *vepřová pečeně* (pork roast).

In this landlocked country, fish options are typically limited to *kapr* (carp) and *pstruh* (trout), prepared in a variety of ways and served with potatoes or fries. Vegetarians can go for the delicious *smažený sýr s bramborem* (fried cheese with potatoes) or default to *čočka s vejci* (lentils with fried egg).

Side Dishes: You'll typically need to order your garnishes separately (except for meal-on-plate lunch specials). The most common sides are *knedlíky* (bread dumplings), *zelím* (cabbage), and *bramborem* (potatoes). *Šopský salát,* like a Greek salad, is usually the best salad option. The server will bring it with the main dish, unless you specify that you want it before.

Dessert: Consider the following for *moučník* (dessert): *lívance* (small pancakes with jam and curd), *palačinka* (crêpes served with fruit or jam), or z*mrzlinový pohár* (ice-cream sundae). All over Prague's Old Town, you'll find kiosks selling a treat called *trdlo* or *trdelník.* This is a long ribbon of dough wrapped around a stick, slowly cooked on a rotisserie, then rolled in cinnamon, sugar, or other toppings. Try to get one that's still warm, rather than one wrapped in plastic—it makes a big difference.

Beverages: No Czech meal is complete without a cup of coffee. Espresso has become the norm in recent years, and locals drink it with added water and cream on the side. Water comes bottled and generally costs more than beer (tap water is not usually served). Czech mineral waters (*minerálka*) have a high mineral content. Bohemia is beer country, but Moravians prefer wine and *slivovice* (SLEE-voh-veet-seh)—a plum brandy. *Medovina* ("honey wine") is mead.

OLD TOWN

Eateries here can be touristy and expensive. I've sought out more reasonable local options (see map, page 158).

❶ **$$ Restaurace u Provaznice** ("By the Ropemaker's Wife") Czech classics, famously good "pig leg" with horseradish and Czech mustard, on a peaceful lane a block from the bottom of Wenceslas Square.

Provaznická 3, +420 224 232 528

❷ **$$ U Medvídků** ("By the Bear Cubs") Bright, noisy, touristy, flagship beer hall of the Czech Budweiser, a block toward Wenceslas Square from Bethlehem Square.

Na Perštýně 7, +420 736 662 900

❸ **$ U Zlatého Tygra** ("By the Golden Tiger Pub") Proverbial Czech pub, locals line up for good, authentic pub grub and a great (noisy) atmosphere (daily from 15:00).

A block off Karlova at Husova 17, +420 222 221 111

❹ **$ Restaurace u Betlémské Kaple** Behind Bethlehem Chapel; peaceful, woody, and spacious; cheap lunch deals and fish specialties.

Betlémské Náměstí 2, +420 222 221 639

❺ **$$$$ Hotel u Prince Terasa** Atop the five-star hotel facing the Astronomical Clock, rooftop terrace with great view, open-air grill, overpriced, servers can be rude, great for a drink at sunset.

Staroměstské Náměstí 29, +420 737 261 842, www.terasauprince.com

❻ **$$ Restaurace Mlejnice** ("The Mill") Fun little pub two blocks from the Old Town Square; traditional specials, hearty salads, and modern Czech plates; reservations smart for dinner.

Kožná 14, +420 224 228 635, www.restaurace-mlejnice.cz

❼ **$$ Lokál** Good-quality Czech classics, retro design celebrates the hungry and thirsty working class, reservations smart.

Dlouhá 33, +420 734 283 874, https://lokal-dlouha.ambi.cz

❽ **$$$$ V Zátiší** Untraditional and imaginative; delicate deer, duck, and fish swim in carefully calibrated sauces (Mon-Sat lunch and dinner, Sun dinner only).

Liliová 1, +420 222 221 155

❾ **$$$ Kogo Havelská** Modern takes on traditional Italian cuisine; pasta, fish, and meats paired with seasonal ingredients.

Havelská 29, +420 224 210 259

⑩ $$$ Indian Jewel Authentic restaurant offering Indian classics, vegetarian options, good-value lunch specials on weekdays.

Rybná 9, +420 725 107 059

---

⑪ $ James Joyce Irish Pub Local favorite serving basic pub grub, fish and chips, curries; worn wooden floors and dingy walls transport you to Dublin.

U Obecního Dvora 4, +420 224 818 851

---

⑫ $$ La Casa Blů One of the last student bastions in the Old Town, cheap lunch specials, Mexican plates, Staropramen beer, greenish mojitos (daily, Sun from 14:00).

On the corner of Kozí and Bílkova, +420 224 818 270

---

⑬ $$$ Kolkovna Big and woody yet modern, a bit overpriced, serves mix of Czech and international cuisine—ribs, salads, cheese plates.

Across from Spanish Synagogue at V Kolkovně 8, +420 224 819 701

---

⑭ $$$ Alforno Focacceria Italiana Low-key slice of Italy, splurge on fancy fish and meat dishes or opt for affordable pasta, weekday lunch specials.

Široká 25, +420 224 818 322

---

⑮ $$$ King Solomon Restaurant Traditional Jewish dishes in a handsome setting; roasted, grilled, and braised meats; fixed-price *menu* offers range of dishes for a good price, Fri and Sat Shabbat meals by reservation only.

Široká 8, +420 224 818 752, www.kosher.cz

NEW TOWN

Less atmospheric neighborhood best for pub grub, international cuisine, or Art Nouveau décor (see map, page 158).

⑯ $$ Restaurace u Pinkasů Basic Czech pub grub in traditional interior or delightful garden.

Jungmannovo Náměstí 16, +420 221 111 152

---

⑰ $$ Café Louvre Classic atmosphere, simple tables, army of young waiters serving up Czech and vegetarian dishes, lunch specials.

Národní 22, +420 724 054 055

---

⑱ $ Knedlín ("The Dumpling Village") Tiny place that serves 20 kinds of dumplings, both sweet and savory; minuscule tables.

Národní 24, +420 702 214 518

---

⑲ $$ Kantýna Cross between butcher's shop and modern canteen, wide selection of freshly made soups, salads, and desserts.

A block off the middle of Wenceslas Square at Politických Vězňů 5

20 **$$ Pivovarský Dům** ("The Brewhouse") Offers variety of fresh beers, classic Czech dishes, inviting interior; reservations recommended in the evenings.
Lípová 15, +420 296 216 666, www.pivo-dum.cz

21 **$$$ Municipal House** Three eateries amid the Art Nouveau splendor: dressy Kavárna Obecní Dům café with light, pricey meals, great atmosphere, and bad service; expensive and formal Restaurace Obecní Dům with modern Czech cuisine; overpriced beer cellar filled with tour groups.
Kavárna +420 222-002-763, Obecní Dům +420 222-002-777

22 **$$ Grand Café Orient** Upstairs in the Cubist House of the Black Madonna, decorated with a Cubist flair; good-value menu of sandwiches, salads, vanilla squares, and other desserts; balcony seating.
Near the Powder Tower at Ovocný Trh 19, +420 224 224 240

23 **$$ Kavárna Slavia** Former hangout café for Prague's literary elite, Art Deco interior, a bit tired but iconic status, fun stop for a coffee.
Across from National Theater at Smetanovo Nábřeží 2, +420 224 218 493

LESSER TOWN

Characteristic eateries on cobblestoned lanes, handy for a bite before or after your castle visit (see map, page 160).

24 **$$ Malostranská Beseda** Imaginative menu of traditional Czech dishes, vegetarian fare and fresh fish; three settings: ground-floor restaurant, café, or packed beer hall.
In former Town Hall at Malostranské Náměstí 21, +420 257 409 112

25 **$$ Lokál U Bílé Kuželky** ("By the White Bowling Pin") Best bet for quick, cheap, well-executed Czech classics on this side of the river.
From Charles Bridge, right at U Tří Pštrosů Hotel, Míšeňská 12, +420 257 212 014

26 **$$ St. Martin** Quintessential neighborhood pub serving inexpensive dishes; burgers, beers, wines from Moravian wineries.
Just above the American embassy at Vlašská 7, +420 257 219 728

27 **$$ Vegan's Prague** Vegan variations on Czech classics as well as Asian fare, gorgeous vistas.
Nerudova 36, +420 735 171 313

28 **$ U Hrocha** ("By the Hippo") Small authentic pub, packed with beer drinkers; serves simple, traditional meals; cash only.
Near Lesser Town Square at Thunovská 10, +420 257 533 389

㉙ **$$ Cukrkávalimonáda** ("Sugar, Coffee, Lemonade") Part restaurant and part patisserie, big salads, made-to-order sandwiches, artful pastries, fresh-squeezed juice (daily until 19:00).

Lázeňská 7, +420 257 225 396

㉚ **$$$ Café Savoy** Viennese-style café mixing French, Austrian, and Czech influences; elegant Art Deco surroundings, weekday lunch specials.

Vítězná 5, +420 731 136 144

㉛ **$$ Petřínské Terasy** Near funicular stop on Petřín Hill, great views from outside terrace, woody seating indoors, traditional menu, cash only.

Petřín 393, +420 257 320 688

CASTLE QUARTER

My listings either boast views or are handy for your castle visit (see map, page 160).

㉜ **$$$ Villa Richter** Surrounded by vineyards, gorgeous city view, serves "street food" paired with vineyard's wine (daily until 19:00).

Near castle exit gate by the Golden Lane, +420 702 282 402

㉝ **$$$ Lobkowicz Palace Café** Three seating options—aim for terrace views; soups, salads, sandwiches, Czech classics (daily until 18:00).

At far end of castle near end of Golden Lane, +420 731 192 281

㉞ **$$ U Labutí** ("By the Swans") Czech food for a good price in tranquil courtyard, just across from the Plague Column on Castle Square.

Hradčanské Náměstí 11, +420 220 511 191

㉟ **$$ Kuchyň** ("Kitchen") Small terrace with great views, serving Czech classics with a modern twist.

Behind Masaryk statue on Castle Square at Hradčanské Náměstí 1, +420 736 152 891

㊱ **$ Kavárna ve Šternberském Paláci** Quiet getaway behind Archbishop's Palace, dishes up soup or goulash with bread and drinks (Tue-Sun until 18:00, closed Mon).

Hradčanské Náměstí 15, +420 703 372 197

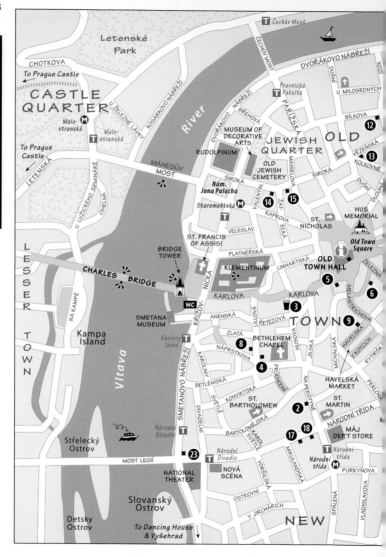

Restaurants in Old & New Towns

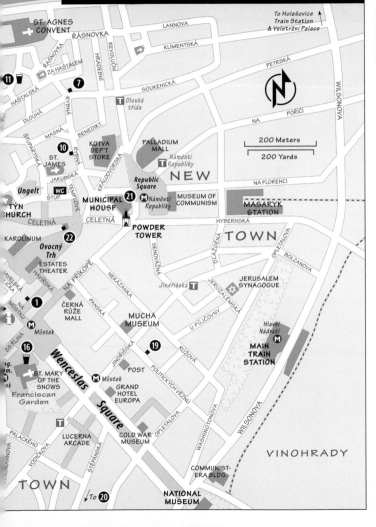

To Holešovice Train Station & Veletržní Palace

ST. AGNES CONVENT

LANNOVA

RÁSNOVKA

KLIMENTSKÁ

RÁSNOVKA

REVOLUČNÍ

HRADEBNÍ

PETRSKÁ

ZA HAŠTALEM

SOUKENICKÁ

11

7

HAŠTALSKÁ

RYBNÁ

Dlouhá třída

NA POŘÍČÍ

WILSONOVA

DLOUHÁ

MASNÁ

BENEDIKT.

ŠTUPARTSKÁ

10

ST. JAMES

RYBNÁ

KOTVA DEP'T STORE

KRÁLODVORSKÁ

PALLADIUM MALL

Náměstí Republiky

NA FLORENCI

JAKUBSKÁ

Ungelt

WC

STUP.

TEMPLOVÁ

Republic Square

N E W

TÝN CHURCH

MUNICIPAL HOUSE

21

Náměstí Republiky

MUSEUM OF COMMUNISM

MASARYK STATION

CELETNÁ

CELETNÁ

POWDER TOWER

HYBERNSKÁ

KAROLINUM

22

Ovocný Trh

T O W N

ESTATES THEATER

NA PŘÍKOPĚ

NEKÁZANKA

SENOVÁŽNÁ

DLÁŽDĚNÁ

OPLETALOVA

BOLZANOVA

HAVELSKÁ

HAVELSKÁ

1

ČERNÁ RŮŽE MALL

PANSKÁ

JERUZALÉMSKÁ

JERUSALEM SYNAGOGUE

Jindřišská

i

Müstek

MUCHA MUSEUM

U PŮJČOVNY

Hlavní Nádraží

28. ŘÍJNA

NA MŮSTKU

MAIN TRAIN STATION

16

Jindřišská

19

RŮŽOVÁ

ST. MARY OF THE SNOWS

Müstek

POST

POLITICKÝCH VĚZŇŮ

WASHINGTONOVA

WILSONOVA

Franciscan Garden

GRAND HOTEL EUROPA

COLD WAR MUSEUM

OPLETALOVA

Wenceslaz Square

PALACKÉHO

LUCERNA ARCADE

ŠTĚPÁNSKÁ

VINOHRADY

VODIČKOVA

COMMUNIST-ERA BLDG.

T O W N

To **20**

NATIONAL MUSEUM

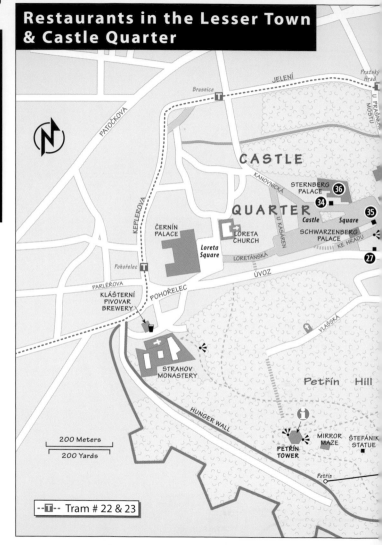

Restaurants in the Lesser Town & Castle Quarter

EATING

--🚋-- Tram # 22 & 23

200 Meters

200 Yards

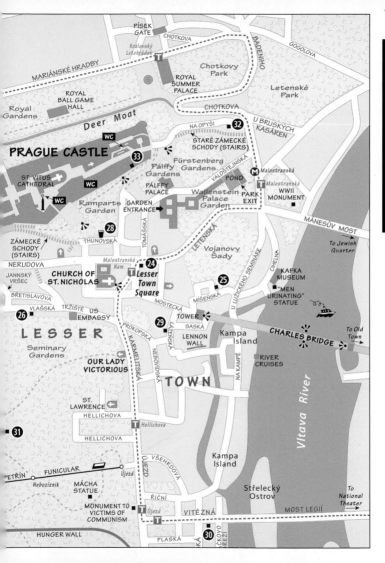

Practicalities

HELPFUL HINTS

Travel Tips

Travel Advisories: Before traveling, check updated health and safety conditions, including restrictions for your destination, at Travel. State.gov (US State Department travel pages) and CDC.gov (Centers for Disease Control and Prevention).

Tourist Information: The Old Town has two TIs: on the **Old Town Square** (in the Old Town Hall, left of the Astronomical Clock; Tue-Sun 9:00-19:00, Mon from 11:00) and around the corner from **Havelská Market** (at Rytířská 12; daily 9:00-19:00). There's also a TI in the Lesser Town at **Petřín Tower** (daily 9:00-20:30, shorter hours off-season). For tourist information in English, dial +420 221 714 714 (Mon-Fri 9:00-17:00) or check Prague.eu.

Hurdling the Language Barrier: The language barrier in the Czech Republic is no bigger than in Western Europe. You'll find that most people in the tourist industry—and just about all young people—speak English well.

Time Zones: The Czech Republic is six/nine hours ahead of the East/West Coasts of the US. For a handy time converter, use the world clock app on your phone or download one (see www.timeanddate.com).

Business Hours: Most stores are open Monday through Friday from 9:00 or 10:00 until 17:00 or 18:00 and Saturday morning until lunchtime, and closed Sunday. Souvenir shops in the Old Town are open daily until at least 20:00.

Watt's Up: Europe's electrical system is 220 volts, instead of North America's 110 volts. Most electronics (laptops, phones, cameras) and appliances (hair dryers, CPAP machines) convert automatically, so you won't need a converter, but you will need an adapter plug with two round prongs, sold inexpensively at travel stores in the US.

Safety and Emergencies

Emergency and Medical Help: For any emergency service—ambulance, police, or fire—call **112** from a mobile phone or landline. If you get sick, do as the locals do and go to a pharmacist for advice (see "Around Town," next). Or ask at your hotel for help—they'll know the nearest medical and emergency services.

Theft or Loss: The city has more than its share of pickpockets—especially in the train station, on trams, in and near crowded museums, and at places of drunkenness. Keep your valuables—passport and backup cards and cash—in your money belt.

To replace a **passport,** you'll need to go in person to the US Embassy (24-hour line: +420 257 022 000; open Mon-Fri by appointment only, in Prague's Lesser Town below the castle at Tržiště 15; https://cz.usembassy.gov). If your credit and debit cards disappear, cancel and replace them, and report the loss immediately (call these 24-hour US numbers: Visa—+1 303 967 1096, Mastercard—+1 636 722 7111, and American Express—+1 336 393 1111). For more information, see RickSteves.com/help.

Rip-Offs: As in any heavily touristed city, naive tourists can fall victim to con artists. Any time you pay for something with cash, note how much you're handing over and how much you expect back. Count your change.

Around Town

English Bookstore: For a wide selection of translations from Czech, try **Shakespeare and Sons,** one block from the Charles Bridge on the Lesser Town side at U Lužického Semináře 10.

Maps: Google Maps works well here for navigation. A good map

The area by the Old Town Hall is a hub of tourist services and sightseeing options.

Helpful Websites

Prague Tourist Information: Prague.eu

Czech Republic Tourist Information: CzechTourism.com

Passports and Red Tape: Travel.State.gov

Flights: Flights.Google.com (international flights), SkyScanner.com (flights within Europe)

Airplane Carry-on Restrictions: TSA.gov

Train Schedules: Bahn.com

General Travel Tips: RickSteves.com (train travel, rail passes, car rental, travel insurance, packing lists, and more)

of Prague is also helpful. Get one showing tram and Metro lines, plus tiny sketches of the sights, at kiosks and tobacco stands. I also like the *Kartografie Praha* city map.

Pharmacies: You'll find handy pharmacies in the Palladium shopping center on Náměstí Republiky and at Palackého 5 near Wenceslas Square (both open 9:00-18:00). A 24-hour pharmacy is at the Na Františku hospital.

Laundry: A **full-service laundry** is at Karolíny Světlé 11 near Charles Bridge on the Old Town side (Mon-Fri only, +420 721 030 446); another is at Rybná 27 (Mon-Fri only, +420 602 511 695). **Prague Andy's Laundromat** offers self-service (daily, Korunní 14, +420 733 112 693, www.praguelaundromat.cz).

ARRIVAL IN PRAGUE

Main Train Station (Hlavní Nádraží)

Prague's **main train station** ("Praha hl. n." on schedules) serves all international trains; most trains within the Czech Republic, including high-speed SC Pendolino trains; and buses to and from Nürnberg and Munich.

The station is a busy hive of shops and services; posted maps help you find your way. Three parallel tunnels connect the tracks to the arrival hall. The main hall has four Metro entrances in the center.

The one good **ATM** (pink, Unicredit Bank) is under the stairs across from the main ticket office. Avoid the blue-and-yellow Euronet ATMs, which have bad rates. **Lockers** are in the corner under the stairs on the right, and a **Billa supermarket** is in the corner under the stairs to the left.

To get the best prices and to ensure you get on your preferred train (some can sell out), buy ahead online at Idos.Idnes.cz. Tickets for Czech Railways (České Dráhy) trains are also sold at CD.cz. To purchase in person, the **CD ticket office**—marked *ČD Centrum*—is in the middle of the main hall under the stairs.

To get from the train station to your hotel, you have several options.

On Foot: Most hotels I list in the Old Town are within a 20-minute walk of the train station. Exit the station into a small park, walk through the park, and then cross the street on the other side. Head down Jeruzalémská street to the Jindřišská Tower and tram stop, walk under a small arch, then continue slightly to the right down Senovážná street. At the end of the street, you'll see the Powder Tower—the grand entry into the Old Town—to the left. Alternatively, Wenceslas Square in the New Town is a 10-minute walk—exit the station, cross the park, and walk to the left along Opletalova street.

By Metro: The Metro is easy. The entrance is right inside the station's main hall—look for the red *M* with two directions: *Háje* or *Letňany*. To purchase tickets from the machine by the Metro entrance, you'll need a credit card. Validate your ticket in the yellow machines *before* you go down the stairs to the tracks.

To get to hotels in the Old Town, take the Letňany-bound red line from the train station to Florenc, then transfer to the yellow line

Invest in a good map with transit lines.

Explore by following pictographic signs.

The busy Main Train Station has Old World class and modern tourist services.

(direction: Zličín) and get off at either Náměstí Republiky, Můstek, or Národní Třída; these stops straddle the Old Town. For details on Prague's public transit, see "Getting Around Prague," later.

By Taxi or Uber: The fair metered rate into the Old Town is about 200 Kč; if your hotel is farther out or across the river, it should be no more than 300 Kč. Avoid the "official" taxi stand that's marked inside the station: These thugs routinely overcharge arriving tourists. To get an **honest cabbie,** exit the station's main hall through the big glass doors, then cross 50 yards through a park to Opletalova street. A few taxis are usually waiting there in front of Hotel Chopin, on the corner of Jeruzalémská street. Or call a taxi (operators speak English; AAA Taxi—+420 222 333 222; City Taxi—+420 257 257 257). Before getting into a taxi, always confirm the maximum price to your destination, and make sure the driver turns on the meter. For more pointers on taking taxis, see page 171.

Uber works the same way it does at home and typically costs less than a taxi. Drivers pick up from the small parking lot next to platform 1B.

By Tram: The nearest tram stop is to the right as you exit the station (about 200 yards away). Tram #9 (headed away from railway tracks) takes you to the neighborhood near the National Theater and the Lesser Town but isn't useful for most Old Town hotels.

Václav Havel Airport

Prague's modern, tidy, user-friendly Václav Havel Airport is located 12 miles (about 30 minutes) west of the city center. Terminal 2 serves destinations within the EU (no passport controls); Terminal 1 serves everywhere else. The airport has ATMs (avoid the change desks), transportation services (such as city transit and shuttle buses), kiosks selling city maps, and a TI (airport code: PRG, www.prg.aero).

Getting between the airport and downtown is easy. Leaving either airport terminal, you have several options.

Budget: Take the airport express (AE) bus to the main train station (60 Kč, runs every half-hour daily about 6:00-21:00, 40 minutes, look for the *AE* sign in front of the terminal and pay the driver, www.cd.cz). From the station, you can take the Metro, hire a taxi or Uber, or walk to your hotel.

Moderate: Prague Airport Transfers offers 24-hour shuttle and taxi service (door-to-door shared taxi-290 Kč/person; +420 222 554 211 from Czech Republic or +420 516 340 3070 from US, www.prague-airport-transfers.co.uk). Uber usually costs about half the price of a taxi; drivers pick up in the parking lot facing Terminal 1.

Expensive: Book a yellow AAA taxi through their office in the airport hall—you'll get a 50 percent discount coupon for the trip back. AAA taxis wait in front of exit D at Terminal 1 and exit E at Terminal 2 (metered rate, generally 600 Kč to downtown). For reliable transport and fair rates, try Mike's Chauffeur Service, listed later.

GETTING AROUND PRAGUE

You can walk nearly everywhere. Brown street signs (in Czech, but with helpful little icons) direct you to tourist landmarks. It's worth figuring out the public-transportation system, which helps you reach farther-flung sights (Prague Castle, Vyšehrad, and so on). The Metro is slick, the trams fun, and Uber quick and easy.

By Tram and Metro

The trams and Metro (plus buses) use the same tickets:

- 30-minute **short-trip ticket** (*krátkodobá*), which allows as many transfers as you can make in a half-hour—30 Kč
- 90-minute **standard ticket** (*základní*)—40 Kč
- **24-hour pass** (*jízdenka na 24 hodin*)—120 Kč
- **3-day pass** (*jízdenka na 3 dny*)—330 Kč

Since Prague is a great walking town, most find that buying a few individual tickets works better than a pass. Tickets are available from several outlets. The official **PID Lítačka app** allows you to purchase mobile tickets, which you can either activate immediately or save to use later. To use a mobile ticket, scan the QR code as you board.

Paper tickets are sold at **hotels, newsstand kiosks,** and **machines at Metro stops.** Be sure to validate your ticket as you get on the tram or bus, or as you enter the Metro station, by sticking it in the yellow machine, which stamps a time on it. Inspectors routinely ambush ticketless riders (including tourists) and fine them 1,000 Kč on the spot.

For trams and buses, tickets are also sold **on board** at a red ticket machine in the middle of the tram car or bus (tap-to-pay cards only). Tickets bought from these onboard machines have the time printed on them and don't need to be validated.

You can find more information and a route planner in English at DPP.cz.

Trams: Trams run every few minutes in the daytime (a schedule is posted at each stop). Navigate by signs that list the end stations. At the platform, a sign lists all the stops for each tram in order. Remember that trams going one direction leave from one platform, while trams going the other direction might leave from a different platform nearby. When the tram arrives, open the doors by pressing the green button.

Learn a few handy tram lines.

Use tram #22/23 for a self-guided city tour.

Newer trams have electronic signs that show either the next stop (*příští*) or a list of upcoming stops. Recorded announcements state the name of the current stop, followed by the name of the stop coming up next.

These lines are especially useful: **Tram #22** (or #23, the retro 1960s version) is practically made for sightseeing, connecting the New Town with the Castle Quarter, with several convenient stops in between (see my "Welcome to Prague Self-Guided Tram Tour" on page 120); **trams #17** and **#18** go along the south bank of the river, connecting Vyšehrad and the New and Old Town embankments; **tram #2** connects Malostranská (on the castle side of the river) with stops along the Old Town embankment, then cuts inland along Národní Třída and south to Charles Square; and **trams #9** and **#24** are helpful for traveling across town from the main train station and the Wenceslas Square and Republic Square stops.

Metro: The three-line Metro system is handy and simple but doesn't always get you right to the tourist sights (landmarks such as the Old Town Square and Prague Castle are several blocks from the nearest Metro stops). The Metro closes at midnight, but nighttime tram routes (identified with white numbers on blue backgrounds at tram stops) run all night at 30-minute intervals. Although it seems that all Metro doors lead to the neighborhood of Výstup, that's simply the Czech word for "exit."

By Uber and Taxi

While Prague is fraught with rip-off taxis, it's well served by Uber. If you're comfortable with Uber at home, it works the same way here, and you can generally get a ride within five minutes with no fuss and at about half the taxi fare.

Legitimate local **taxi** rates are cheap: Drop charge starts at 40 Kč, per-kilometer charge is around 30 Kč, and waiting time per minute is about 6 Kč. These rates are clearly marked on the door, so be sure the cabbie honors them. Also insist that cabbies turn on the meter and that it's set at the right tariff, or *"sazba"* (usually but not always tariff #1). There's no extra charge for calling a cab—the meter starts only after you get in. Tip by rounding up; locals never tip more than 5 percent.

Have a ballpark idea of what your ride will cost. Figure about 150-200 Kč for a ride between landmarks within the city center (for example, from the main train station to the Old Town Square, or from the Charles Bridge to the castle). Even the longest ride in the center should cost under 300 Kč.

To improve your odds of getting a fair metered rate, call for a cab (or ask someone at your hotel or restaurant to call for you), rather than hailing one on the street. **AAA Taxi** (+420 222 333 222) and **City Taxi** (+420 257 257 257) are the most likely to have English-speaking staff and honest cabbies. Hailing a passing taxi usually gets you a decent but slightly higher price. Avoid cabs waiting at tourist attractions and train stations; these are far more likely to be crooked.

If a cabbie surprises you at the end with an astronomical fare, challenge it. Point to the rates on the door. Get your hotel receptionist to back you up. Pull out your phone and threaten to call the police. (Because of legislation to curb dishonest cabbies, the police will stand up for you.) Or simply pay what you think the ride should cost and walk away—300 Kč (about $15) should cover you for a long ride anywhere in the center.

Mike's Chauffeur Service is a reliable, family-run company with fair and fixed rates around Prague and beyond. Mike and his colleagues all speak English (+420 602 224 893, www.mike-chauffeur.cz, mike.chauffeur@cmail.cz).

By Bike

Prague's network of bike paths makes bicycles a feasible option for exploring the center and beyond (see https://mapa.prahounakole.cz for a map). Two bike-rental shops are located near the Old Town Square: **Praha Bike** (Dlouhá 24, +420 732 388 880, www.prahabike.cz) and **City Bike** (Králodvorská 5, +420 776 180 284, www.citybike-prague.com). They also rent e-bikes and organize guided bike tours.

By Car

You won't want or need to drive within compact Prague, but a car can be handy for exploring the countryside. All the biggies have offices in Prague (check each company's website or ask at the TI).

Tipping

Tipping in the Czech Republic isn't as automatic and generous as it is in the US, but some general guidelines apply.

Restaurants: At Czech restaurants that have a waitstaff, service is generally not included; it's common to round up the bill after a good meal (about 10 percent).

Taxis: For a typical ride, round up your fare a bit (for instance, if the fare is 180 Kč, pay 200 Kč).

Services: For local guides, private drivers, or others who spend several hours with you and significantly improve the quality of your trip, a healthy tip (of around 10 percent) is not extravagant. In general, if someone in the tourism or service industry does a good job for you, a small tip of about 50 Kč is appropriate...but not required. If you're not sure whether (or how much) to tip, ask a local for advice.

MONEY

The Czech Republic is a member of the European Union but continues to use its traditional currency, the Czech crown (*koruna,* abbreviated Kč): 20 Czech crowns (Kč) = about $1. To roughly convert prices in crowns to dollars, divide by 2 and drop the last digit. Check Oanda. com for the latest exchange rates.

You'll use your **credit card** for purchases both big (hotels, advance tickets) and small (little shops, food stands). A "tap-to-pay" or "contactless" card is widely accepted and simple to use. Check to see if you already have—or can get—a tap-to-pay version of your credit card (look on the card for the tap-to-pay symbol—four curvy lines). Make sure you know the numeric four-digit PIN for each of your cards, both debit and credit. Request it if you don't have one, as it may be required for some purchases.

Use a **debit card** at ATMs (called *Bankomats*) to withdraw a small amount of local cash. While many transactions are by card these days, cash can help you out of a jam if your card randomly doesn't work and can be useful to pay for things like tips and local guides. Keep backup cards and cash safe in a **money belt.**

ATMs work just like at home.

The *koruna* is worth about a nickel.

At self-service payment machines (such as transit-ticket kiosks), US cards may not work. In this case, look for a cashier who can process your card manually—or pay in cash.

STAYING CONNECTED

Making International Calls

From a Mobile Phone: Phone numbers in this book are presented exactly as you would dial them from a US mobile phone. For international access, press and hold 0 (zero) to get a + sign, then dial the country code (420 for the Czech Republic) and phone number.

From a US Landline to Europe: Replace + with 011 (US/Canada access code), then dial the country code (420 for the Czech Republic) and phone number.

From a European Landline to the US or Europe: Replace + with 00 (Europe access code), then dial the country code (420 for the Czech Republic, 1 for the US) and phone number. For more phoning help, see HowToCallAbroad.com.

Using Your Phone in Europe

Sign up for an international plan. To stay connected at a lower cost, sign up for an international service plan through your carrier. Most providers offer a simple bundle that includes calling, messaging, and data.

Use free Wi-Fi whenever possible. Unless you have an unlimited-data plan, save most of your online tasks for Wi-Fi. Most accommodations in Europe offer free Wi-Fi, and many cafés offer hotspots for customers. You may also find Wi-Fi at TIs, city squares, major museums, public-transit hubs, and airports, and aboard trains and buses.

Save large-data tasks for Wi-Fi. If your included data is slow or metered, wait until you're on Wi-Fi to Skype or FaceTime, download apps, stream videos, or do other megabyte-greedy tasks. Using a navigation app such as Google Maps over a cellular network can require lots of data, so download maps when you're on Wi-Fi, then use the app offline.

Use Wi-Fi calling and messaging apps. Skype, FaceTime, and Google Meet are great for making free or low-cost calls or sending texts over Wi-Fi worldwide. WhatsApp is especially popular with Europeans and is often the easiest way to communicate with guides, drivers, or other local contacts.

RESOURCES FROM RICK STEVES

Begin your trip at RickSteves.com: This book is just one of many in my series on European travel. I also produce a public television series, *Rick Steves' Europe,* and a public radio show, *Travel with Rick Steves*. My mobile-friendly website is *the* place to explore Europe in preparation for your trip. You'll find thousands of fun articles, beautiful photos, videos, and radio interviews; a wealth of money-saving tips; travel news dispatches; a video library of travel talks; our latest guidebook updates (RickSteves.com/update); and the free Rick Steves Audio Europe app with audio tours of Europe's top sights. You can also follow me on Facebook, Instagram, and X.

Packing Checklist

Clothing

- ❑ 5 shirts: long- & short-sleeve
- ❑ 2 pairs pants (or skirts/capris)
- ❑ 1 pair shorts
- ❑ 5 pairs underwear & socks
- ❑ 1 pair walking shoes
- ❑ Sweater or warm layer
- ❑ Rainproof jacket with hood
- ❑ Tie, scarf, belt, and/or hat
- ❑ Swimsuit
- ❑ Sleepwear/loungewear

Money

- ❑ Debit card(s)
- ❑ Credit card(s)
- ❑ Hard cash (US $100-200)
- ❑ Money belt

Documents

- ❑ Passport
- ❑ Other required ID: Vaccine card, entry visa, etc.
- ❑ Driver's license, student ID, hostel card, etc.
- ❑ Tickets & confirmations: flights, hotels, trains, rail pass, car rental, sight entries
- ❑ Photocopies of important documents
- ❑ Insurance details
- ❑ Guidebooks & maps
- ❑ Extra passport photos
- ❑ Notepad & pen
- ❑ Journal

Toiletries

- ❑ Soap, shampoo, toothbrush, toothpaste, floss, deodorant, sunscreen, brush/comb, etc.
- ❑ Medicines & vitamins
- ❑ First-aid kit
- ❑ Glasses/contacts/sunglasses
- ❑ Face masks & hand sanitizer
- ❑ Sewing kit
- ❑ Packet of tissues (for WC)
- ❑ Earplugs

Electronics

- ❑ Mobile phone
- ❑ Camera & related gear
- ❑ Tablet/ebook reader/laptop
- ❑ Headphones/earbuds
- ❑ Chargers & batteries
- ❑ Plug adapters

Miscellaneous

- ❑ Day pack
- ❑ Sealable plastic baggies
- ❑ Laundry supplies
- ❑ Small umbrella
- ❑ Travel alarm/watch

Optional Extras

- ❑ Second pair of shoes
- ❑ Travel hairdryer
- ❑ Disinfecting wipes
- ❑ Water bottle
- ❑ Fold-up tote bag
- ❑ Small flashlight & binoculars
- ❑ Small towel or washcloth
- ❑ Tiny lock

Czech Survival Phrases

The emphasis in Czech words usually falls on the first syllable—but don't overdo it, as this stress is subtle. A vowel with an accent (á, é, í, ú, ý) is held longer. The combination ch sounds like the guttural "kh" sound in the Scottish word "loch." The uniquely Czech ř (as in Dvořák) sounds like a cross between a rolled "r" and "zh"; in the phonetics, it's "zh." Here are a few English words that all Czechs know: super, OK, pardon, stop, menu, problem, and no problem.

Hello. (formal)	Dobrý den.	**doh**-bree dehn
Hi. / Bye. (informal)	Ahoj.	**ah**-hoy
Do you speak English?	Mluvíte anglicky?	mloo-**vee**-teh ahn-**glits**-kee
Yes. / No.	Ano. / Ne.	**ah**-noh / neh
I don't understand.	Nerozumím.	**neh**-roh-zoo-meem
Please / You're welcome. / Can I help you?	Prosím.	**proh**-seem
Thank you.	Děkuji.	**dyeh**-kwee
Excuse me. / I'm sorry.	Promiňte.	proh-**meen**-teh
Good.	Dobře.	**dohb**-zheh
Goodbye.	Nashledanou.	**nah**-skleh-dah-noh
one / two / three	jeden / dva / tři	**yay**-dehn / dvah / tzhee
hundred / thousand	sto / tisíc	stoh / **tee**-seets
How much?	Kolik?	**koh**-leek
local currency	koruna (Kč)	koh-**roo**-nah
Where is...?	Kde je...?	guh-**deh** yeh
...the train station	...nádraží	**nah**-drah-zhee
...the bus station	...autobusové nádraží	ow-toh-boo-soh-veh **nah**-drah-zhee
...the tourist information office	...turistická informační kancelář	too-rih-stit-skah **een**-for-mahch-nee **kahn**-tseh-lahzh
...the toilet	...vécé	**veht**-seh
men / women	muži / ženy	**moo**-zhee / **zheh**-nee
At what time...?	V kolik...?	f**koh**-leek
...does this open / close	...otevírají / zavírají	oh-teh-vee-rah-yee / **zah**-vee-rah-yee
today / tomorrow	dnes / zítra	duh-**nehs** / **zee**-trah

In a Czech Restaurant

I'd like to reserve... (said by a man)	Rád bych zarezervoval... rahd bikh **zah**-reh-zehr-voh-vahl
I'd like to reserve... (said by a woman)	Ráda bych zarezervovala... **rah**-dah bikh **zah**-reh-zehr-voh-vah-lah
...a table for one / two.	...stůl pro jednoho / dva. stool proh **yehd**-noh-hoh / dvah
The menu (in English), please.	Jídelní lístek (v angličtině), prosím. **yee**-dehl-nee **lee**-stehk (**fahn**-gleech-tee-nyeh) **proh**-seem
Service is / isn't included.	Spropitné je / není zahrnuto. **sproh**-pit-neh yeh / **neh**-nee zah-har-noo-toh
breakfast / lunch / dinner	snídaně / oběd / večeře **snee**-dahn-yeh / **ohb**-yeht / **veh**-cheh-sheh
appetizers	předkrmy **pzhehd**-krih-meh
bread / cheese / sandwich	chléb / sýr / sendvič khlehb / seer / **sehnd**-veech
soup / salad	polévka / salát poh-**lehv**-kah / **sah**-laht
meat / poultry / fish	maso / drůbež / ryby **mah**-soh / **droo**-behzh / **rih**-bih
fruit / vegetables	ovoce / zelenina **oh**-voht-seh / **zeh**-leh-nyee-nah
dessert	dezert **deh**-zehrt
(tap) water	voda (z kohoutku) **voh**-dah (**skoh**-hoht-koo)
mineral water	minerální voda **mih**-neh-rahl-nyee **voh**-dah
carbonated / not carbonated (spoken)	s bublinkami / bez bublinek **sboob**-leen-kah-mee / behz **boo**-blee-nehk
(orange) juice	(pomerančový) džus (**poh**-mehr-ahn-choh-vee) "juice"
coffee / tea	káva / čaj **kah**-vah / chai
wine / beer	víno / pivo **vee**-noh / **pee**-voh
red / white	červené / bílé **chehr**-veh-neh / **bee**-leh
glass / bottle	sklenka / lahev **sklehn**-kah / **lah**-hehv
Cheers!	Na zdraví! nah zdrah-**vee**
More. / Another.	Více. / Další. **veet**-seh / **dahl**-shee
The same.	To samé. toh **sah**-meh
The bill.	Účet. **oo**-cheht
tip	spropitné **sproh**-pit-neh
Delicious!	Výborné! **vee**-bohr-neh

INDEX

Start your trip at

Our website enhances this book and turns

Explore Europe

At ricksteves.com you can browse through thousands of articles, videos, photos and radio interviews, plus find a wealth of money-saving travel tips for planning your dream trip. And with our mobile-friendly website, you can easily access all this great travel information anywhere you go.

TV Shows

Preview the places you'll visit by watching entire half-hour episodes of *Rick Steves' Europe* (choose from all 100 shows) on-demand, for free.

ricksteves.com

your travel dreams into affordable reality

Radio Interviews

Enjoy ready access to Rick's vast library of radio interviews covering travel tips and cultural insights that relate specifically to your Europe travel plans.

Travel Forums

Learn, ask, share! Our online community of savvy travelers is a great resource for first-time travelers to Europe, as well as seasoned pros.

Travel News

Subscribe to our free Travel News e-newsletter, and get monthly updates from Rick on what's happening in Europe.

Classroom Europe®

Check out our free resource for educators with 500 short video clips from the *Rick Steves' Europe* TV show.

Audio Europe™

Pack Light and Right

Gear up for your next adventure at ricksteves.com

Light Luggage

Pack light and right with Rick Steves' affordable, custom-designed rolling carry-on bags, backpacks, day packs and shoulder bags.

Accessories

From packing cubes to moneybelts and beyond, Rick has personally selected the travel goodies that will help your trip go smoother.

Shop at ricksteves.com

Rick Steves has

Save time and energy

This guidebook is your independent-travel toolkit. But for all it delivers, it's still up to you to devote the time and energy it takes to manage the preparation and logistics that are essential for a happy trip. If that's a hassle, there's a solution.

Rick Steves Tours

A Rick Steves tour takes you to Europe's most interesting places with great guides and small groups.

great tours, too!

with minimum stress

We follow Rick's favorite itineraries, ride in comfy buses, stay in family-run hotels, and bring you intimately close to the Europe you've traveled so far to see. Most importantly, we take away the logistical headaches so you can focus on the fun.

Join the fun

This year we'll take thousands of free-spirited travelers—nearly half of them repeat customers—along with us on four dozen different itineraries, from Ireland to Italy to Athens. Is a Rick Steves tour the right fit for your travel dreams? Find out at ricksteves.com, where you can check seat availability and sign up.

Europe is best experienced with happy travel partners. We hope you can join us.

See our itineraries at ricksteves.com

A Guide for Every Trip

BEST OF GUIDES
Full-color guides in an easy-to-scan format, focusing on top sights and experiences in popular destinations

Best of England
Best of Europe
Best of France
Best of Germany

Best of Ireland
Best of Italy
Best of Scotland
Best of Spain

COMPREHENSIVE GUIDES
City, country, and regional guides printed on Bible-thin paper. Packed with detailed coverage for a multi-week trip exploring iconic sights and more

Amsterdam &
  the Netherlands
Barcelona
Belgium: Bruges, Brussels,
  Antwerp & Ghent
Berlin
Budapest
Central Europe
Croatia & Slovenia
England
Florence & Tuscany
France
Germany
Great Britain
Greece: Athens &
  the Peloponnese
Iceland

Ireland
Istanbul
Italy
London
Paris
Portugal
Prague & the Czech Republic
Provence & the French
  Riviera
Rome
Scandinavia
Scotland
Sicily
Spain
Switzerland
Venice
Vienna, Salzburg & Tirol

Many guides are available as ebooks.

POCKET GUIDES
Compact guides for shorter city trips

Amsterdam	Italy's Cinque Terre	Prague
Athens	London	Rome
Barcelona	Munich & Salzburg	Venice
Florence	Paris	Vienna

SNAPSHOT GUIDES
Focused single-destination coverage

Basque Country: Spain & France
Copenhagen & the Best of Denmark
Dublin
Dubrovnik
Edinburgh
Hill Towns of Central Italy
Krakow, Warsaw & Gdansk
Lisbon
Loire Valley
Madrid & Toledo
Milan & the Italian Lakes District
Naples & the Amalfi Coast
Nice & the French Riviera
Normandy
Northern Ireland
Norway
Reykjavík
Rothenburg & the Rhine
Sevilla, Granada & Southern Spain
St. Petersburg, Helsinki & Tallinn
Stockholm

CRUISE PORTS GUIDES
Reference for cruise ports of call

Mediterranean Cruise Ports
Scandinavian & Northern European
   Cruise Ports

TRAVEL SKILLS & CULTURE
Greater information and insight

Europe 101
Europe Through the Back Door
Europe's Top 100 Masterpieces
European Christmas
European Easter
European Festivals
For the Love of Europe
Italy for Food Lovers
Travel as a Political Act

PHRASE BOOKS & DICTIONARIES

French
French, Italian & German
German
Italian
Portuguese
Spanish

PLANNING MAPS

Britain, Ireland & London
Europe
France & Paris
Germany, Austria & Switzerland
Iceland
Ireland
Italy
Portugal
Scotland
Spain & Portugal

PHOTO CREDITS

Avalon Travel
Hachette Book Group
555 12th Street
18th floor
Oakland, CA 94607

Printed in Malaysia for Imago
Third Edition. First printing September 2024

ISBN 978-1-64171-625-3

For the latest on Rick's talks, guidebooks, tours, public television series, and public radio show, contact Rick Steves' Europe, 130 Fourth Avenue North, Edmonds, WA 98020, +1 425 771 8303, RickSteves.com, rick@ricksteves.com.

Rick Steves' Europe
Managing Editor: Jennifer Madison Davis
Editorial Group Manager: Cathy Lu
Editors: Glenn Eriksen, Tom Griffin, Suzanne Kotz, Rosie Leutzinger, Teresa Nemeth, Jessica Shaw, Carrie Shepherd, Chelsea Wing
Contributor: Gene Openshaw
Creative Director: Sandra Hundacker
Maps & Graphics: Orin Dubrow, David C. Hoerlein, Lauren Mills, Mary Rostad

Avalon Travel
Senior Editor and Series Manager: Madhu Prasher
Associate Managing Editors: Jamie Andrade, Sierra Machado
Copy Editor: Jennifer Malnick
Proofreader: Nikki Ioakimedes
Indexer: Claire Splan
Production & Typesetting: Rue Flaherty
Cover Design: Kimberly Glyder Design
Interior Design: Darren Alessi
Maps & Graphics: Kat Bennett

Let's Keep on Travelin'

Your trip doesn't need to end.

Follow Rick on social media!